BRIA CLOUGH

FIFTY DEFINING FIXTURES

Marcus Alton

AMBERLEY

In memory of my Dad, David Alton

First published 2017

Amberley Publishing
The Hill, Stroud
Gloucestershire, GL5 4EP

www.amberley-books.com

British Library Cataloguing in Publication Data.
A catalogue record for this book is available from the British Library.

ISBN 978 1 4456 4930 6 (print)
ISBN 978 1 4456 4931 3 (ebook)

Origination by Amberley Publishing.
Printed in the UK.

Contents

Introduction

When Brian Clough recalled what he got for Christmas in 1962, the response was typically to the point: 'I got done.' More specifically, it was his knee that got 'done' as it crunched into the goalkeeper's shoulder in a challenge for a loose ball. It was a life-changing and career-defining moment. Clough had been an outstanding goalscorer but the injury effectively ended his playing career. Football was his world and while the dramatic events of that Boxing Day match dealt a cruel blow to his ambitions of playing regularly in the top flight, it opened the door to a managerial career that reached the pinnacle of club football. This book is the first to focus on a collection of key matches, spanning nearly four decades, which tell the incredible Clough story.

As a centre forward, Clough was absolutely brilliant, scoring the fastest 250 goals in Football League history. Although most of those goals were in Division Two, his talent and unrivalled ability to hit the back of the net could not be doubted. Even in those early days, he was a controversial and outspoken character. After scoring five in a 9-0 win he said the added responsibility of being captain had held him back. Yet he was rewarded with just two England caps. The story behind those two appearances is told later in this book.

As a manager, Clough was a genius. His man-management skills were unrivalled. His brand of attractive, clean and decisive football won admirers around the world, even from the supporters of opposition clubs. When Clough signed a new contract on the Baseball Ground pitch, in front of the television cameras, he clambered onto the terraces to ask the Sheffield United fans who had arrived early to be quiet while the ceremony took place. To their credit, the visiting fans hushed those who still wanted to make a noise and, when it was over, they began chanting 'Cloughie for England'. Only Brian Clough could have that kind of influence. It was fitting that nearly twenty-one years later, it was visiting United fans who joined the home supporters singing Clough's name in his final League match at the City Ground.

Clough was the original Special One, long before José Mourinho came along. On the day of his appointment at Nottingham Forest, the Sports Editor of the *Nottingham Evening Post*, Harry Richards, was quick to herald the 'special' arrival. 'Playing morale is low and support has eroded,' wrote Mr Richards. 'Something special was required to change the sombre picture and we think that something special has arrived in the person of Clough.' Fast forward to August 2016 and Clough was named as one of the all-time great bosses who invented modern football. *Four Four Two* magazine included him in an illustrious list that featured Bill Shankly and Sir Matt Busby. It described Clough as 'the Ultimate Motivator' and said Mourinho was following in the pioneering manager's footsteps. Shortly before Clough died, he remarked that he liked the look and sound of the Portuguese boss, who was then at Chelsea, especially when it came to ensuring the discipline of players. 'Some people have compared him to the way I went about managing and I can see the similarities,' he said. 'I was almost as good-looking as him when a young manager and I had even more to say than him.' Clough was certainly the king of the one-liners. The actor who portrayed Old Big 'Ead in a highly successful tribute play, the late Colin Tarrant, told me he reckoned that Clough could have been a successful stand-up comedian, such was his timing and delivery of those unforgettable remarks. When he was asked for his opinion of Manchester United opting out of the FA Cup for one season to play in the World Club Championship, his verdict prompted more than a few chuckles: 'Manchester United in Brazil? I hope they all get bloody diarrhoea.'

The former chairman of the Nottingham Forest Supporters Club and Brian Clough Statue Fund in Nottingham, Paul Ellis, has no doubts that the achievements of Brian Howard Clough will never be surpassed. 'If you read some reports these days, you would think that football never existed before the Premier League was introduced,' says Paul. 'But what Clough managed to achieve as a player and then a manager was incredible. His goalscoring exploits were absolutely outstanding. He then took two small-town teams and lifted them from the doldrums of Division Two to the top of the tree. In the case of Nottingham Forest, he transformed them beyond recognition after they were promoted as also-rans in third place. In their first season in the top flight they won the league which included the European champions at the time, Liverpool. Not only that, they went on to win the European Cup twice in successive seasons. When a team manages to achieve that in the modern era, only then can comparisons be made with what Clough achieved. But we will probably be waiting a long, long time.' It was therefore fitting that Clough's European Cup-winning teams were inducted into the National Football Museum's Hall of Fame in 2016, something that was long overdue. Clough himself had been inducted in the Hall of Fame, but sadly after he had died.

In the programme for Clough's testimonial match at Sunderland in 1965, a number of leading journalists at the time paid tribute. One of the comments still resonates today. Vince Wilson of the *Sunday Mirror* wrote, 'You could praise him, you could slam him – but you could never ignore Brian Clough. The club, the fans, the game and the sporting Press are the poorer for his absence.' That sentiment was to be felt by fans and journalists many years later, not only when he retired but after he sadly passed away in September 2004.

Clough's own Roy of the Rovers story is illustrated in this book through some of the key matches of his playing and managerial career, spanning nearly four decades. To put it simply, in the terms of one of his famous quotes (plucked from a regional television interview and then given worldwide publicity through my tribute website brianclough.com), Cloughie may not have been the best goalscorer or the greatest manager that football has ever known, but he was in the top one.

* * *

Cloughie legend Martin O'Neill once said that he had been asked in a television interview if he could sum up Brian Clough's genius in three words. 'He would have been insulted if he was summed up in three volumes,' added O'Neill. In the same way, attempting to summarise the great man's career in fifty matches would probably have sparked a similar response. 'Fifty matches? Blow me, more like 500, young man,' he might have said. It has certainly been a very tough task and this compilation contains by no means the only games that define his playing and managerial career. But I hope you agree it focuses on some of the key matches that tell the incredible Clough story and, at least, opens up debate. After all, football is all about opinions. I had a list that was far longer than fifty, but you have to draw the line somewhere.

Some might argue that you could include Nottingham Forest's abandoned game against Southampton back in February 1977. The Reds were losing 1-0 when the match was called-off due to fog only two minutes into the second half. When the match was replayed, Forest won 2-1 and secured a vital two points in their search for promotion to the old Division One. Those two points proved to be hugely important as they grabbed promotion by finishing in third place in Division Two. But football is full of ifs and buts. Singling out fifty matches across a glittering career spanning some thirty-eight years, I felt it was far more important to include the Reds' triumph in the Anglo-Scottish Cup in the same season. Yes, it was a minor cup competition, but Clough himself knew how important it was for his players to get a taste of success by lifting a trophy. Years later, reflecting on his fifteenth anniversary at Forest, he said, 'I got one of my biggest kicks in beating Leyton Orient to win the Anglo-Scottish Cup at a time when we were trying to get out of the Second Division.' And who could argue with the man himself?

Like my other Clough books, this one has been a labour of love and I would like to thank a number of people for their assistance. First of all, a big thanks to the helpful staff at the main libraries in Middlesbrough, Hartlepool, Sunderland, Nottingham and Derby, where I spent many hours searching through the archives. I should also mention Andy Ellis for his Derby County statistics, Barnsley FC historian Grenville Firth and the late Ken Smales for his statistical history of Forest. In addition, archived copies of newspapers such as the *Sunderland Echo*, *Middlesbrough Evening Gazette*, *Hartlepool Mail*, *Nottingham Evening Post* and *Derby Evening Telegraph* have been great sources of information. It was also marvellous to hear the personal memories of Ron Stevenson, Paul Ellis, Mike Simpson, Rich Fisher, Colin Shields and Richard Hallam. Others who deserve huge thanks include Sophie Stewart and Mike Bettison at the BBC and the team at Amberley Publishing, including Alan Murphy and Jenny Stephens. From my own personal point of view, I must thank my Mum, Margaret, for her wonderful support and help in putting this book together, especially during a memorable trip to the north east. To my wife Sarah, thanks for your incredible patience and unwavering support – once again you have been a great source of strength and inspiration. During the writing of this book, sadly my Dad passed away and it is with that in mind that part of my proceeds will go to Diabetes UK.

Many years ago, my Dad was invited into Brian Clough's office. It was a moment he would never forget (my Dad that is!). He had been waiting in the car park of Nottingham Forest's City Ground to ask the Master Manager to sign a book he was planning to give me for Christmas. Clough could not have been kinder that day. He asked Dad to join him in his office and signed the book, 'To Marcus, Be Good, Brian Clough.' Over a number of weeks, Dad made sure he got the signatures of all the Forest players at the time, including names like Trevor Francis, Peter Shilton and Kenny Burns, as well as assistant manager Peter Taylor and trainer Jimmy Gordon. It was quite a collection of signatures. Not only that, Dad also tracked down many former players. By then some of them were running their own businesses. On Christmas morning, when I unwrapped that book by John Lawson that told the history of Forest, I could not believe that all those famous names had signed the book especially for me. It is still a cherished possession.

Decades later, Dad joined me at a special dinner in which Cloughie was the guest speaker. We both thoroughly enjoyed the evening and at the end of it I was keen to get a photograph with my sporting hero. Brian had time for everyone who wanted to speak to him, even though he was due to have left the event much earlier. I think it took him half an hour to reach the exit, as admirers asked for a quick word, an autograph or a photograph. After a quick chat with Brian as he made his way towards the door, I hastily handed Dad the camera and the resulting photograph is a permanent reminder of a wonderful evening. I was so pleased with it that it was used as the cover picture of my first book about Cloughie. Dad was very proud of that – as he often gently reminded me! I'm pleased he always admired my Cloughie books, as well as the work I instigated to get a statue of the great man in Nottingham. At the statue unveiling he enjoyed talking to Brian's brother Joe and we often reflected on that memorable day. Sometimes Dad would give copies of my books as presents to friends and would let me know who he would like them signed to. Well, Dad, this one's especially for you. I hope you'll be proud again – and thank you for being such an inspiration.

Division Two
Middlesbrough 1 Barnsley 1
17 September 1955

No matter how much success I've had as a football manager – and I have won a thing or two – nothing will compare with the pleasure I got from my playing days.

Brian Clough joined his home town club Middlesbrough as an amateur in 1951. He had played regional football with local sides Billingham Synthonia and Great Broughton, where he was in the team alongside three of his brothers (Joe, Bill and Des) and his brother-in-law Sid during their 1952/53 championship-winning season. Middlesbrough offered him a full-time contract in May 1955, paying him the equivalent of £7 a week. He lived just a short distance from Middlesbrough's Ayresome Park ground, in the house he grew up in on Valley Road. His walk to the ground would take him through Albert Park, where he had played football, cricket and tennis when he was a boy. A statue of Brian was unveiled in the park in May 2007.

Clough set an incredible goalscoring record at Middlesbrough, with a ratio of almost one goal per game, with 204 goals in 222 matches between 1955 and 1961. But he recalled that, for a time, he was way down the pecking order when it came to the manager's choice for centre forward. He was behind Charlie Wayman, Ken McPherson and Doug Cooper. After scoring fifteen goals in nine games for the reserves, Clough did enough to earn an appearance for the first team. He made his debut at the age of twenty against Barnsley in September 1955.

Middlesbrough: Ugolini, Bilcliff, Stonehouse, W. C. Harris, Robinson, R. W. Dicks, Delapenha, J. C. Scott, Clough, Fitzsimons, A. J. Mitchell.
Barnsley: Hough, Swift, Betts, Wood, Spruce, Jarman, Kaye, Lumley, Brown, Graham, Bartlett.

Attendance: 24,960

The inclusion of Clough in the Middlesbrough team was the only change to the side that had drawn at Bury the previous week. Despite the goalscoring prowess he would show later in his playing career, this was a fairly low-key debut by his standards. In the first minute he headed the ball to Arthur Fitzsimons and a shot flashed across the face of the goal. Clough continued to cause problems for the visitors' defence and at one point had the ball in the Barnsley net, but it was disallowed. Writing in the *Middlesbrough Evening Gazette*, Cliff Mitchell reported, 'Towards the interval Middlesbrough stepped up the pressure but luck was certainly against them in one fine move. Scott, though fouled, got the ball into the centre and Clough netted.' Mitchell went on to explain that although there was a roar from the crowd, the referee pointed to the edge of the penalty area and awarded a free-kick to the home side instead. Lindy Delapenha took the kick but Barnsley keeper Harry Hough made the save. Middlesbrough continued to attack and won several corners, but the Barnsley defence stood firm. Cliff Mitchell wrote that the Barnsley forwards had been 'little more than spectators for a long time' but 'Boro could not make their possession pay and the score remained goalless at half-time.

The home side started the second half in the same way they had finished the first, with Clough trying to make an impression on his debut. Bert Mitchell got the ball into the middle and Clough headed to Joe Scott, but the inside right's header was saved easily by Hough. Soon afterwards, the visiting 'keeper was called into action again and saved a low drive by Delapenha. Barnsley hit back when 'Boro defender Dick Robinson slipped and Arthur Kaye sent the ball to the far post where Frank Bartlett sliced a shot wide. Middlesbrough won two corners within a minute and from the second a Clough header was saved by Hough. Two further headers from the striker were again saved following corners. Clough also headed the ball down to Joe Scott who tried to score, but the ball hit the side netting.

It seemed it just wasn't going to be Middlesbrough's day. That feeling appeared to be justified when Barnsley took a surprise lead after fifty-six minutes. They broke away and won a free-kick when full-back Derek Stonehouse obstructed Kaye. The winger, who would play for Middlesbrough a few years later, sent a strong shot towards the goal and Brown helped it into the net. The home side continued to press forward but the frustrations remained. Hough saved a Delapenha header and Fitzsimons went close with a first-time shot. Then, at long last, the pressure paid off and Clough helped Middlesbrough to equalise with eight minutes to go. He passed to Fitzsimons, whose 20-yard drive beat the diving Hough. In his second autobiography *Walking on Water*, Clough recalled that Harry Hough's name alone summed-up the toughness and honesty of the 'keeper. Clough said,

As you might imagine, he was as tough as a tree, solid as a rock – that I can vouch for because, as a centre forward, I knew that when he clattered you there was no room for doubt; you had the bruises to remind you for weeks.

Writing in the *Middlesbrough Evening Gazette* on the Monday after the Barnsley match, Cliff Mitchell said he had not made his mind up about Clough. He said the young forward still had a lot to learn and was finding it difficult to bridge the gap between the North Eastern League and Division Two. But Mitchell said Clough had done enough in the game to suggest he would make the adjustment and he described the debut as one of promise. He admitted that Clough could have received far more support from his teammates, even though he was well marshalled by the opposing centre half. Fans were urged to be patient and to show a little more understanding. Summing up Clough's performance, Mitchell's verdict was inspired: 'I think he'll be among the goals for Borough's first team in the near future.'

Division Two
Nottingham Forest 0 Middlesbrough 4
10 November 1956

When Brian Clough popped into this world on 21 March 1935, the knack of scoring goals came with him. When the midwife held me by the ankles and smacked my bum, I didn't cry – I yelled 'one-nil.'

Clough scored his first goal for Middlesbrough on 8 October 1955 in a 4-3 win at home to Leicester City. In ten first team appearances during the 1955/56 season, he scored three goals. But his goals-to-games ratio soon gathered pace the following season when manager Bob Dennison made him the first choice centre forward. In the 1956/57 season, Clough scored thirty-eight goals in forty-one League appearances. His first hat-trick for Middlesbrough came away at Nottingham Forest, the club he would lead to its greatest achievements as manager. Forest had started the season in impressive form and were unbeaten in their first seven games; they went on to win promotion to Division One that season. But Clough played a vital role in inflicting one of their ten defeats. In the matchday programme introducing the visitors, the description of Clough highlighted his potential impact. It said,

> Definitely one of 'Boro's young players to keep an eye on for the future. Appeared in the first team last season but with only moderate success. However, this season he has gained a permanent berth and is rewarding the club by scoring very regularly. With sixteen goals he is well among the division's leading marksmen.

Nottingham Forest: Nicholson, Hutchinson, Thomas, Morley, McKinlay, Burkitt, Small, Bailey, Higham, Lishman, Imlach.
Middlesbrough: Taylor, Barnard, Stonehouse, Harris, Robinson, Dicks, Delapenha, McLean, Clough, Fitzsimons, Burbeck.

Attendance: 20,862

Middlesbrough were 1-0 up at half-time thanks to Clough's first goal, scored after forty-four minutes. Lindy Delapenha broke down the right and the resulting cross was headed out of Nicholson's reach by Clough. The second half began with Forest on the attack and it looked like they might get an equaliser. But Clough added a second on sixty-eight minutes, despite Forest having more of the possession. Clough broke free of McKinlay to receive a pass from Burbeck and sidestepped Nicholson firing the ball home. The 'Boro forwards were given plenty of chances thanks to a succession of passes from Bill Harris and Ronnie Dicks. In the *Middlesbrough Evening Gazette*, Cliff Mitchell praised Derek McLean, describing him as 'the lad who gave Forest's defence its toughest time'. There was a solid display from the visitors' defence, including great saves from goalkeeper Peter Taylor, who would later become Clough's managerial assistant as well as a key friend and confidante. Taylor had a trick up his sleeve when Forest were awarded a penalty earlier in the game. As Jack Burkitt prepared to take the kick at the Trent end, Taylor left his line to talk to Burkitt in an effort to disrupt his concentration. As he did this, a linesman alerted the referee to an earlier offence and after consultation the penalty decision was rescinded and 'Boro were awarded a free-kick. Clough completed his hat-trick after seventy-nine minutes following good work by Fitzsimons. Among those in the crowd that day was Clough fan Mike Simpson, who had arrived early to get a good view at the front of the Trent end. Mike, who was twelve years old, was with his dad and some friends and remembers that rain affected the playing conditions. He recalled,

> It was a really wet afternoon and that made it difficult for the players to control the ball. In such tricky conditions, Brian's skills were clear to see among the Middlesbrough players. It wasn't easy yet he was still able to complete an impressive hat-trick. The roar of the 'Boro supporters after each of his goals was tremendous. You could tell he was something special, he had a fantastic instinct to score goals. He had that knack of knowing exactly where the ball would be passed to him and where the goalkeeper would be positioned.

Middlesbrough's fourth goal was blasted into the net by Fitzsimons after Nicholson had beaten away a shot by Clough. 'It's wonderful, absolutely wonderful,' was Clough's reply after being asked by Cliff Mitchell how it felt to score his first hat-trick in the League. Clough went on to praise his teammates:

> Lindy Delapenha gave me the first goal, Ronnie Burbeck the second and Arthur Fitzsimons the last. Don't forget that, Cliff. And don't forget the work Derek McLean put in – what a fighter he is – and how the lads in defence held out

when Forest were on top. I couldn't have done a thing without the lads playing with me. It's grand to play in the side these days because everyone is fighting and helping you all they can.

The following season, Clough continued his superb goalscoring record for Middlesbrough in Division Two. He hit four in the first home victory of the campaign, while also setting up another for Ron Burbeck, as his team beat Doncaster Rovers 5-0. Cliff Mitchell described him as 'a brilliant prospect' who possessed 'the priceless gift of marksmanship'. He said fans now recognised Clough as a player worthy to follow in the tradition of the great 'Boro centre forwards of the past. The 1957/58 season saw him score forty goals in forty League games.

Division Two
Middlesbrough 9 Brighton 0
23 August 1958

Scoring goals was a way of life for me ... at the time I lived for nothing else.

Brian Clough's strong personality was already having an impact at Middlesbrough when he was made captain for the 1958/59 season. Even in these early days, he was not afraid to speak his mind, on and off the pitch. On matchday his boots certainly did the talking. He scored five goals in his first game as skipper. The local press described it as something of a 'baptism of fire' for newly promoted Brighton, while concluding that it was one of the most convincing victories in 'Boro's history. Clough had passed a late fitness test on a thigh injury to ensure he could lead the team out for 'Boro's first match of the new season.

Middlesbrough: Taylor, Bilcliff, Robinson, Harris, Phillips, Walley, Day, McLean, Clough, Peacock, Holliday.
Brighton & Hove Albion: Hollins, Tennant, Ellis, Bertolini, Whitfield, Wilson, Gordon, Shepherd, Sexton, Foreman, Howard.

Attendance: 32,367

There was a cheer from the crowd when Clough approached the centre of the pitch to toss-up with the Brighton captain Glen Wilson. It was a sign of things to come when Clough won the toss and chose to kick towards the Holgate end. The match, as the scoreline indicates, was very much a one-sided affair. The visitors battled as much as they could, but were generally outclassed. The local newspaper said Derek McLean had run himself into the ground creating chances for his teammates. Middlesbrough's opening goal came within just five minutes of kick-off and was one of two penalties scored by Bill Harris. Brighton's left-back Syd Ellis had handled the ball. Clough made it 2-0 after fifteen minutes. He latched onto a pass from Eddie Holliday, evaded the advancing goalkeeper

Dave Hollins and slotted the ball into the net from a tight angle. Alan Peacock scored the third, chesting the ball down before hammering it into the net. Moments later, a stunning first-time shot by Clough went just over the bar and brought an excited reaction from the crowd. A great shot by Brighton's captain, Wilson, forced Peter Taylor into action in the Middlesbrough goal. But the home side added a fourth before the half-hour mark thanks to Harris' second penalty. Clough made it 5-0 with a tap-in just before half-time.

In the second half, Middlesbrough continued where they had left off in the first. Goals six and seven were scored by Clough who hit a first-time shot into the net for his fourth goal of the match after an hour. A header from Peacock made it 8-0 before Clough completed the rout after controlling a pass from McLean with eight minutes left. Afterwards, Brighton manager Billy Lane said, 'I don't think we can possibly meet a better team in the Second Division. Anyway, I hope not!' Clough, who offered his sympathy to Brighton's goalkeeper, was reported to have had a twinkle in his eye as he said that the added responsibility of being captain had held him back. In the *Evening Gazette*, Cliff Mitchell wrote that if Clough was overlooked by the England selectors this season, then a lot of people from Middlesbrough (and Brighton) would want to know why. Clough scored forty-three goals for Middlesbrough in the 1958/59 season, including three more against Brighton in 6-4 victory. He even grabbed a goal on his wedding day in April 1959, in a 4-2 win over Orient. But Middlesbrough's defensive problems meant they could not win promotion. There were also issues in the dressing room, with nine members of the first team signing a 'round-robin' to have Clough removed as captain. They were unhappy with his outspoken comments, especially about the defence. But his annoyance about how many goals were being conceded was understandable when, despite scoring three of Middlesbrough's six goals in a match against Charlton, they let in six goals themselves and came away with a draw.

International Match
Wales 1 England 1
17 October 1959

No sooner had I begun tucking into a breakfast of bacon and beans than I spilled them into my lap!

It was only a matter of time before Brian Clough earned his first international cap. In addition to his outstanding goalscoring record for Middlesbrough, he had scored for the England 'B' and Under-23 sides. If that was not enough, all the goals in the Football League's 5-0 win over the Irish League in September 1959 came from a young man called Clough. Following that victory in Belfast, Middlesbrough's assistant secretary and former England centre forward George Camsell told the local press,

> I am delighted with Clough's success. Everyone here at Ayresome Park is thrilled that he has done so well. Five goals take some scoring against any opposition, believe me. We can't see anything to stop Brian getting that first full England cap now.

That cap, one of only two he was to earn, came at Ninian Park where he and his Middlesbrough teammate Edwin Holliday made their full international debuts. Writing his regular column for the *Evening Gazette*, Clough revealed that he found out about his selection for England at eleven o'clock on Monday 12 October, following Middlesbrough's 1-1 draw with local rivals Sunderland the previous Saturday. By half past two on the Tuesday he was involved in a practice match for England against Chelsea. He telephoned his article through to the *Gazette*'s offices from the team hotel in Porthcawl. 'For Edwin and myself, I am sure these last few days have been among the happiest of our lives,' said Clough, who also disclosed that Holliday had become the comedian of the group. But there was not much for Clough to laugh about when he spilt his breakfast of bacon and beans into his lap while eating with his colleagues. He admitted that for a naïve lad from Middlesbrough, this represented something of a crisis as he did not have a spare pair of trousers. The former England player Tom Finney (later to be Sir Tom) came to the rescue and arranged for the trousers to be cleaned and returned to Clough within a few hours. Brian admitted he was in awe of Finney and he never forgot the kindness he showed that day. Nevertheless, that incident indicated the nervousness with which the young Middlesbrough player approached his first match for the England senior team. It seems hard to believe now, given how self-confident he became in later life, but Clough admitted he felt vulnerable as England prepared at the team hotel. He was quoted at the time as saying he wanted to succeed not only for his own sake but for the wonderful Middlesbrough supporters who had always cheered him on. He said he did not want to let anyone down.

Middlesbrough fans felt that Clough's inclusion in the team was long overdue. As a result, the anticipation on Teesside was palpable. Brian's dad, Joe, was part of a group of forty people who travelled overnight by coach from Middlesbrough to Cardiff. They were members of the Wilton ICI Polythene Maintenance Social Section, where Joe worked. A larger group of 'Boro fans, totalling more than 150, travelled by train during the night. They gave up the chance to see their top of the table clash with Aston Villa, a match in which Clough's goalscoring skills were missed as 'Boro went down 1-0 at Villa Park. Readers' letters published by the local newspaper also summed up the sense of excitement about Clough's international debut. 'Jack D' from Middlesbrough wrote, 'At last Brian Clough has got the cap he should have had more than a year ago. How on earth they have left him out for so long has been the eighth wonder of the world.' Another correspondent feared that Clough would not get the right type of service from certain teammates. When Clough and Holliday walked into the visitors' dressing room they found a pile of telegrams wishing them good luck.

The England side featured a crop of youngsters as the selectors attempted to make preparations for the 1962 World Cup in Chile. Highlights of the match were shown on a *Sports Special* on BBC television that night, a few hours after the regular Saturday instalment of *Juke Box Jury*. But the afternoon did not hit the right note for Clough, who was playing alongside Bobby Charlton and Jimmy Greaves. The headline in the *Evening Gazette* declared that Clough had been starved of service, as a last-minute goal by the Welsh centre forward Graham Moore salvaged a draw for the home side.

Wales: Kelsey, Williams, Hopkins, Crowe, Nurse, Sullivan, Medwin, Woosnam, Allchurch, Jones C., Moore.
England: Hopkinson, Howe, Allen, Clayton, Smith, Flowers, Connelly, Greaves, Clough, Charlton, Holliday.

Attendance: 62,500

There was heavy rain before kick-off and the wet conditions made it difficult for the players. The *Gazette*'s Cliff Mitchell described Edwin Holliday as England's best forward. But his Middlesbrough teammate had a frustrating time. 'Brian Clough, unhappily but not unexpectedly, received wretched support,' wrote Mitchell. He said Clough had distributed the ball intelligently to both wings and his colleagues in midfield, 'but he waited in vain for a return pass'. England's goal came within half-an-hour as Kelsey could only deflect a close-range drive and Greaves cracked the ball into the net. Mitchell concluded that Clough should be given another chance to shine. On the evidence of his 'excellent distribution alone' he must retain his place, he said. There was still a belief that the new-look England side, when it settled down, could become a force in world football. At the same time, Clough could play an important part in the revival. But, as several letters to the *Evening Gazette* suggested, Clough would need to see more of the ball in order to make his mark. Stan Gibson wrote, 'Clough did a lot of good work and held the line well and if Charlton and Greaves had parted with the ball a few times instead of trying to score themselves more goals might have resulted.'

International Match
England 2 Sweden 3
28 October 1959

It must be every schoolboy's dream to play at Wembley – and why not!

The England selectors and manager Walter Winterbottom showed faith in both Clough and his teammate Holliday by keeping both of them in the side to face Sweden at Wembley, just a few days after the match against Wales. The two players joined Middlesbrough and England trainer Harold Shepherdson as they travelled by train to London from the north east. The weight of expectation on Clough's shoulders was greater than ever and he was desperate to impress. It was his first appearance at Wembley and, writing many years later, he admitted that although it was the realisation of an ambition, the idea of playing there was overtaken by fear. In an uncharacteristic comment, perhaps showing a surprising element of self-doubt, he said, 'You start telling yourself you must do well, hope that you don't miss chances and pray that you do yourself justice … they are the things that go through your mind.'

England: Hopkinson, Howe, Allen, Clayton, Smith, Flowers, Connelly, Greaves, Clough, Charlton, Holliday.
Sweden: Nyholm, Bergmark, Axbom, Jonsson, Johansson, Parling, Thillberg, Borjesson, Berndtsson, Simonsson, Salomonsson.

Attendance: 80,000

Clough's memories of being a player at Wembley were not especially happy. He recalled walking into the England dressing room and thinking it was nothing like the 'homely, comfortable' place he was used to at Ayresome Park. The matchday programme, costing one shilling, featured Jimmy Greaves on the back page in an advertisement for Bovril. Its beefy taste was said to keep him at the top of his form. Unfortunately for Clough, it was a game that left a bad taste. Sweden made the first attack of the game and England were quickly in danger when Flowers attempted to pass the ball back to the goalkeeper. The ball rolled too slowly for Hopkinson, but just as Sweden's centre forward Simonsson ran in to try to latch onto it, Smith intervened in time. England responded with several attacks in which Clough played a part. He sent John Connelly away on the right and received the return pass before slipping the ball inside for Charlton. The Manchester United player sliced his shot wide.

There was some initial optimism when Clough set up the opening goal for Connelly after eight minutes. Then Clough went agonisingly close to scoring. His shot hit the woodwork and rebounded across the goal line. Stranded on the ground, Clough was unable to force the ball over the line. The match report in the *Evening Gazette* described how only 'a couple of inches' separated the 'Boro player from his first goal for England. Goalkeeper Nyholm managed to turn around and grab the ball. In the second half, Sweden not only equalised but took the lead and the home crowd began to jeer. Once again, as in the match against Wales, Clough was said to be starved of service. When he did get another chance, from a Greaves cross, his header hit the bar. Shortly afterwards, an unmarked Salomonsson drove the ball past Hopkinson to increase Sweden's lead to 3-1. Charlton got a goal back for England after eighty-two minutes.

Clough later reflected that Walter Winterbottom had made a mistake by getting the balance of the team wrong. The 'Boro player believed that he, Greaves and Charlton were too similar in their style of play. 'It didn't work, it couldn't work,' Clough reflected, 'but it was his job to find a way of producing a combination that made best use of us.' Clough revealed that the disappointment he and his teammates felt was forgotten briefly when they became stranded in a lift at the London hotel they were staying in. He was one of four players trapped on the fourth floor for around ten minutes while they waited for an engineer to get them out. Reflecting on the defeat, described by one Swedish newspaper as 'The Miracle at Wembley', the press in the north east said Clough had not failed. He simply had not been given the opportunity to fail or to succeed. The match against Sweden was to be Clough's second and final England cap. In some ways, the disappointment he felt after the game may have helped to fuel his anger and frustration at missing out on the England manager's job many years later, when he was the best candidate for the position and the people's choice.

Division Two
Charlton Athletic 6 Middlesbrough 6
22 October 1960

You tend not to forget a scoreline like that...

There is a chapter in Brian Clough's second autobiography entitled 'Goals That Counted For Nothing'. It focuses on his frustration that while he was regularly scoring more than forty goals a season for Middlesbrough, the side was letting in too many at the other end. A team with a goalscorer as prolific as Clough should have been promoted, but they stayed in Division Two. No match could sum up his despair about the situation more than the twelve-goal thriller at Charlton in which he completed a hat-trick, only for 'Boro to concede a late equaliser. After a 3-3 draw at Plymouth and a 4-4 draw at Leeds, this result was described by the *Evening Gazette* as the 'Daddy' of them all. The newspaper's reporter Cliff Mitchell wrote, 'The crowd, kept to small proportions because of the heavy rain, was drunk with goals.' He described 'Boro's forwards as playing brilliantly, with Clough hitting his most lethal form.

Charlton: Duff, Sewell, Townsend, Hinton, Tocknell, Lucas, Lawrie, Edwards, Leary, Werge, Summers.
Middlesbrough: Appleby, Bilcliff, McNeil, Harris, Thomson, Yeoman, Waldock, McLean, Clough, Peacock, Burbeck.

Attendance: 10,064

Middlesbrough were the more threatening side in the opening minutes, with Clough involved in several early attacks. As the pressure from the visitors continued, a fierce shot from Clough was saved by Willie Duff. Charlton responded well and could have taken the lead when the former 'Boro winger Sam Lawrie sent Eddie Werge through on his own. But the inside left's close-range shot went over the bar. Another shot by Werge was saved by Bob Appleby before

Werge eventually put the home side in front after thirteen minutes following a cross from Johnny Summers. Two minutes later, Middlesbrough equalised as Peacock headed the ball towards the far post and Clough controlled it before hitting a tremendous shot into the roof of the net. Burbeck made it 2-1 to the visitors just two minutes later, before Charlton equalised in the twenty-first minute. Shortly afterwards, there was disappointment when a Clough effort was disallowed due to an earlier foul by Ray Yeoman. A defensive mix-up involving Appleby and Thomson allowed Charlton to take the lead again, before 'Boro drew level at 3-3 thanks to McLean. Clough scored again on the half-hour, with what Cliff Mitchell described as one of his 'old-time specials' finishing in the corner of the net. But the visitors' defensive weaknesses were exposed again just before the interval when Edwards headed home for Charlton. The half-time score was 4-4 and both sides were reported to have received 'a wonderful ovation' from the crowd as they left the pitch.

The excitement continued after the break, with Burbeck giving Middlesbrough the lead before Clough completed his hat-trick to make it 6-4. But Charlton responded with another goal from Edwards, for the second hat-trick of the game, and then equalised in the eighty-ninth minute when Summers floated the ball towards goal and Appleby misjudged it. The ball went over the goalkeeper's arms and into the net, prompting hundreds of youngsters to run onto the pitch. Cliff Mitchell concluded that 'Boro's 'rearguard' had let the side down, although there were exceptional circumstances due to the muddy conditions. Clough was left exasperated. In his autobiography *Walking on Water* he reflected, 'You tend not to forget a scoreline like that, not even me – a hat-trick to my name away from home and we still couldn't win. I'd been trying my darndest, busting a gut.'

On the train journey home to the north east, Clough shouted to a group of his teammates who were playing cards, 'If I can manage to get four goals next week, you never know, we might even win.' The response that was shouted back to him was along the lines that if the team had a centre forward who was mobile enough to make himself available for the ball, they may stand a chance. There was certainly no love lost between Clough and some of his colleagues. A group of them had already signed a 'round-robin', or petition, against Clough's appointment as captain. Whenever the players gathered at Rea's Café in Middlesbrough after training, there would be a group sitting on one side, while Clough and the teammates who supported him sat on the other side. Years later, looking back at the on-field problems, Clough acknowledged that 'Boro's defensive frailties taught him an important lesson for when he became a manager. He would know that all good sides were built on strong defences. Having an effective goalkeeper and centre half was just as important as recruiting a successful goalscorer.

By the end of the 1960/61 season, it was clear that Clough would not be staying at Middlesbrough; he had already made several transfer requests. Eventually the club agreed he could go. In an end-of-season interview published in the *Evening Gazette*, Clough denied the final breach between himself and the club had been caused by any friction with other players. He said that since the trouble of the 'round-robin' had died down, his relationship with his teammates had been quite cordial. Speaking with a managerial-type assessment that would become a key quality in the future, he said he believed that Middlesbrough had possessed the talent to win promotion that season, but that talent had not been 'properly harnessed'. The team had been playing as eleven individuals rather than as a cohesive unit, he said. Clough added that he had not enjoyed playing football 'for a long time' and he thought that the same could be said of other first-team players. 'Now I want to start enjoying it again – somewhere else.' Finally, he was asked if he had a message for the club's supporters. 'Yes I'd like to thank them publicly for all the encouragement they've given in my years at Ayresome Park.' He wanted 'Boro fans to know that he was sorry that he and the rest of the players had been unable to give them what had often been promised: a return to Division One football.

Division Two
Walsall 4 Sunderland 3
19 August 1961

There were occasions when I was downright scared of the man.

When Brian Clough met Sunderland boss Alan Brown for the first time in the summer of 1961, it was a pivotal moment in Clough's career. Not only did it give him a new lease of life as a centre forward, but Brown would become a significant influence. Their first meeting was on a quayside in Southampton, where Brown had gone the 'extra mile' to get his man, who was returning from a Mediterranean cruise with his wife Barbara. Brown was so determined to sign Clough that he approached him as soon as the couple had stepped off the ship. A deal between the two men was agreed straightaway. Clough was signed for around £45,000 and shortly afterwards the Sunderland chairman Syd Collings said, 'I know I am speaking on behalf of the board – and I am confident supporters will agree – when I say I would rather see Sunderland in the First Division with an overdraft than in the Second Division with money in the bank.'

With his emphasis on discipline among players and being the type of manager who spoke his mind, Alan Brown was a mentor for Clough. In later years, good behaviour on and off the pitch would be the hallmark of Brian Clough teams. They would be a favourite among referees who knew they would get no nonsense from players managed by Clough. Brown was a tough taskmaster and when he delivered a telling-off, the player involved would be left in no doubt about who was in charge. Even Clough himself admitted he was afraid of the Sunderland manager. But equally, such was the respect Clough had for his new boss, he would later say he would have run through a brick wall if Brown had ordered him to do so. Those who played for Clough in future years would have similar sentiments. Brown ran the club from top to bottom and Clough realised that if ever he had the opportunity to manage a club himself, it would be the Alan Brown way. As a manager, Clough would copy the idea of going the 'extra mile' to sign certain players, just as Brown had done. Clough went to the homes of Roy McFarland and Archie Gemmill to secure their signatures and turned up at White Hart Lane in order to persuade Dave McKay to sign for Derby from Spurs. Just as Brown detested his players having long hair, Clough recruits were expected to have short, neat hair. One of his first orders to a young John McGovern at Hartlepools was to get his hair cut, 'because you look like a girl'.

By joining Sunderland Clough would be playing alongside a defence he admired and had praised in his newspaper column in October 1959. Their defender Charlie Hurley, he said, was regarded by many as one of the finest centre halves – if not the finest – in the country. Writing in the *Evening Gazette*, he described Hurley's most outstanding quality as being the fact he was known as a 'footballing centre half' who, unlike the majority who played in that position, tried to bring the ball down and then give it to an unmarked teammate. Clough said this quality was worth noting because most centre halves he had ever played against were only focused on one thing: blocking out the centre forward 'at all costs'. Having said that, Clough admitted that Hurley had been so effective during two matches against Middlesbrough that the imposing defender had prevented him from having a kick of the ball during both games. Hurley, capped forty times by Ireland, was shortlisted for the Football Writers' Association Player of the Year award in 1964, only to be denied by a certain Bobby Moore who would captain England's World Cup winners two years later. In 1979, Hurley was named Player of the Century in a special poll of Sunderland fans to mark the club's centenary.

Clough's first game for Sunderland was a friendly against the Danish side Odense. Hurley told him, 'Alright Brian we'll break you in gently with a couple of goals.' Hurley was spot on with his prediction as the new recruit scored twice in a 5-1 win. Clough made his League debut for Sunderland at newly promoted Walsall. In the pocket-sized matchday programme (not much bigger than a packet of cigarettes and from which the Walsall team line-up below is taken) the description of Clough was short and to the point. It said he was bought from neighbours Middlesbrough 'for a big fee' during the close season and added, 'Noted for his consistent scoring season by season. A grand all-round player.' As for Charlie Hurley, the observation was, 'Though big and strong, an outstandingly skilful ball player.' In his programme notes, entitled 'Club Comments and Views', Jim Tatler described the match and Walsall's return to Second Division football as a 'momentous occasion'. Like Sunderland, the club's aim was to win promotion to Division One, he said. Tatler added that the scene was set for possibly the most important season in the club's history. 'Already one Sunday newspaper have written them up as relegation candidates at the end of the season,' he said. 'I have no doubt that all at the club will have something to say about this in a manner more expressive than words.' Walsall had won promotion from the Fourth to the Second Division in successive seasons and it was clear they were approaching the match against Sunderland with a point to prove. And so it turned out. Although Clough scored on his League debut for his new club, he ended up on the losing side.

Walsall: Christie, Palin, Sharples, Hill, McPherson, Dudley, Askey, Hodgkinson, Wilson, Richards, Taylor.
Sunderland: Wakeham, Nelson, Ashurst, Anderson, Hurley, McNab, Hooper, Herd, Clough, Fogarty, Overfield.

Attendance: 18,420

Sunderland changed their strip for the new season, replacing their traditional black shorts with white ones. It was not to be a lucky omen as they began the new campaign with an away defeat to Walsall. According to *Sunderland Echo* correspondent Argus, the home side won the toss and decided to give Sunderland the advantage of a pronounced slope of the pitch in the first half. The visitors' goalkeeper was called into action early in the game when Dudley hit a long pass through the Sunderland defence and Wakeham had to rush from his goal to dive at Wilson's feet. Sunderland responded with several attacks, but Clough was caught offside in one of them. A foul on Clough won Sunderland a free-kick 10 yards outside the Walsall penalty area but Anderson overhit the ball and it went out for a goal kick. According to Argus, Walsall benefitted from a 'lucky break' in the twelfth minute when they won a penalty. McNab tried to tackle Askey and the winger fell to the ground. Richards scored from the spot, sending a low drive to Wakeham's right and into the net. Clough equalised on twenty-one minutes, being in the right place following good work from George Herd. But the match report by Argus said there was little chance of Clough distinguishing himself in such a game. It said, 'He was fiercely marked, poorly supported and, most of the time, quite subdued.' Richards went on to score a hat-trick for Walsall who went behind twice after taking the lead initially. Sunderland's threat was reduced when Herd, one of the visitors' scorers, suffered a thigh strain after half an hour and spent the rest of the match on the wing. Even the usually dependable Hurley was said to be troubled by Wilson's pace and strength. Hooper scored a penalty for Sunderland, but there were plenty of lessons for the visitors to learn from the match. It was followed by a 3-0 defeat at Liverpool. When the Merseyside club came to Sunderland later the same month, Clough scored the only goal in a 4-1 defeat. But his first hat-trick for his new club was just around the corner.

Division Two
Sunderland 3 Bury 0
27 September 1961

Coming to Sunderland was the best thing I ever did.

During his first season with Sunderland, Brian Clough continued to show the same kind of goalscoring form he had demonstrated with such dramatic effect at Middlesbrough. He grabbed thirty-four goals in that first campaign for his new club, including five hat-tricks – the first of which came against Bury. He did not know it at the time, but the opposition from the north-west would have a significant part to play in his future just over a year later. It was against Bury that he would suffer a devastating injury in December 1962. Nevertheless, for this Wednesday night match with a 7.15 p.m. kick-off, the impressive centre forward certainly had his scoring-boots on, during what the local press described as 'a great night for Clough'.

Sunderland: Wakeham, Irwin, Ashurst, Anderson, Hurley, McNab, Hooper, Herd, Clough, Fogarty, Overfield.
Bury: Adams, Gallagher, Conroy, Riggs, Stokoe, Atherton, Holden, Beaumont, Watson, Jackson, Hubbard.

Attendance: 39,893

All three goals were described in the local newspaper as 'brilliantly taken' by Clough, with Harry Hooper playing an important part in creating them. The *Sunderland Echo's* football correspondent, Argus, said the centre forward had a 'storming game' in the middle during a hard-working display. His first goal was a fine header from a Hooper cross just before the half-hour mark. The second came seven minutes later as he turned to beat Bob Stokoe and sent a powerful shot past Frank Adams. In the second half Adams made a great save from a Clough effort and then a shot from George Herd hit the post. Clough completed his hat-trick three minutes from the end. He received a return pass from Hooper, held off two tackles and hit another impressive shot past Adams.

Clough went on to score further hat-tricks that season against Walsall (in the League Cup), Plymouth Argyle, Swansea and Huddersfield Town. That victory at home to Huddersfield on 24 March 1962, just three days after Clough's twenty-seventh birthday, was the first of seven consecutive wins, including victory against his former club, Middlesbrough. Clough scored in all but two of those seven victories and his goal against 'Boro was the only one of the match.

Sunderland went on to beat Southampton, Luton Town, Newcastle United and Rotherham United (twice, home and away), which meant a win over Swansea in the final fixture of the season could secure promotion. Many fans travelled overnight to Wales by train, bus or car, while some arrived by plane. Clough scored with a header to give Sunderland the lead. But Swansea got a second-half equaliser and the game ended in a 1-1 draw, which was not enough to lift the visitors into Division One. 'We gave everything we had,' said captain Stan Anderson, 'and I really thought we were going to make it after that great goal by Brian Clough. But what can you do when luck is against you?' The ball had unfortunately eluded young defender Cecil Irwin on the goal line for Swansea's goal. Leyton Orient pipped Sunderland to the second promotion place by just one point. Nevertheless, there was a feeling that promotion for Sunderland would not be far away.

League Cup: Fifth Round
Sunderland 3 Blackburn Rovers 2
5 December 1962

Sunderland people are beautiful.

If ever there are any doubts about whether Brian Clough would have made a consistently outstanding First Division centre forward at the height of his goalscoring prowess, this match showed his true credentials against top-level opposition. Yes, all but one of his 251 League goals were scored in Division Two, but his overall performance and two goals in this cup tie against Blackburn from Division One indicated that he would have risen to the challenge of playing regularly in the top flight if he had stayed injury-free. The match also reignited hopes that there may have been another international call-up in the pipeline. In order to reach this League Cup quarter-final, Sunderland had beaten Oldham Athletic (7-1), Scunthorpe United (2-0) and Portsmouth (2-1 in a replay). According to the *Sunderland Echo*, Clough's two goals laid the foundation for his team's victory against Blackburn, with the first goal described as 'a magnificent effort which swung the game in their favour'. For Rovers, boasting international players Ronnie Clayton and Mick McGrath, it was a first defeat in eleven matches.

Sunderland: Montgomery, Nelson, Ashurst, Harvey, Hurley, McNab, Hooper, Herd, Clough, Fogarty, Mulhall.
Blackburn: Else, Bray, Newton, Clayton, Woods, McGrath, Ferguson, Lawther, Pickering, Douglas, Ratcliffe.

Attendance: 24,727

Blackburn started the match looking very threatening and took an early lead on a frozen pitch. Bryan Douglas set up the move for former Sunderland centre forward Ian Lawther to strike the ball home from the edge of the penalty area in the fifth minute. But, according to *Sunderland Echo* correspondent Argus, it was the man who replaced Lawther at Sunderland, Brian Clough, who provided 'the biggest thrill of the night' with an impressive goal six minutes later. He held off two challenges, flicked the ball past Matt Woods and went round the defender before hitting a great left-foot shot past Else. When Jimmy McNab headed the home side in front in the twenty-third minute, it was quite clear they meant business. Clough scored his second an hour later, but in between there was, according to Argus, 'a fascinating battle of wits in which both sides made and missed chances'. Only a minute after Clough had made it 3-1, Rovers got back on the scoresheet thanks to an own goal by Len Ashurst and nearly got an equaliser through Lawther in the closing minutes. But Martin Harvey and McNab were said to have outshone the international pairing of Clayton and McGrath while Ashurst and Colin Nelson had the Blackburn wingers firmly under control to help secure a well-deserved victory. The combination of Herd, Clough and Fogarty was described by the local press as 'perfectly balanced'. The match report also had a glowing reference to goalkeeper Jim Montgomery who needed a stitch inserted into a cut above his left elbow after a brave dive in the first half.

Although Clough had helped Sunderland secure a place in the League Cup semi-finals, the devastating injury he suffered three weeks later meant they would have to play without him. Facing Aston Villa, they lost the first leg at home 3-1, with Clough's replacement Nicky Sharkey getting their goal. Due to a major fixture backlog caused by a severe winter, the second leg was not played until 22 April. That game was goalless and Clough-less. Sunderland were knocked out of the League Cup. But the effect of their star centre forward's injury on Boxing Day 1962 would have far more significance than the team's cup disappointment.

Division Two
Sunderland 0 Bury 1
26 December 1962

Suddenly it was as if someone had just turned out the light.

Looking back on this fateful day, Clough described it as the one that changed his life – because it changed the knee joint in his right leg. The tragic injury he suffered came on what he described as 'one of those grey, biting, forbidding days that only the north-east can produce'. It was snowy, sleety and bitterly cold. He said it was 'the kind of day when seagulls flew backwards to stop their eyes watering'. It meant the pitch was rock hard and completely unforgiving when Clough went into the challenge that effectively ended his playing career. Yet the season had begun with so much promise. In the opening League game he had scored twice in a 3-1 win over his former club, Middlesbrough. By the time the festive season came, he had scored the 250th League goal of his career. It was the fastest 250 goals scored by any player in the history of the Football League. Many years later, in retirement, it was still a statistic that generated a huge amount of pride for him.

As fans enjoyed the festivities of Christmas 1962, there is no doubt Clough was in his prime and on course for a record-breaking season that could have brought Sunderland supporters the ultimate gift: promotion to Division One. He went into his twenty-fourth League game of the campaign, against Bury, having scored twenty-four League goals. But it was his determination to add to this tally that led to it all coming to an end far too soon. The superb match report by *Sunderland Echo* football correspondent Argus declared that the club had taken their heaviest blow in years. It was not the end of a thirty-one-game unbeaten run that painted a gloomy picture, he said, but the sad news that the injury that had caused Clough to be stretchered off could keep him out of action for the rest of the season. Unfortunately, the prognosis for the prolific centre forward was to be even worse.

Sunderland: Montgomery, Nelson, Ashurst, Harvey, Hurley, McNab, Davison, Herd, Clough, Fogarty, Mulhall.
Bury: Harker, Threfall, Eastham, Turner, Stokoe, Atherton, Bradley, Griffin, Calder, Jones, Bartley.

Attendance: 42,407

According to the report in the local newspaper, Sunderland could have been 3-0 up in the first eighteen minutes, with Clough playing a key role in all three chances. He was said to have given Bury's player-manager Bob Stokoe 'the runaround'. Clough mishit an angled drive before a close-range shot was parried over the bar by goalkeeper Chris Harker. The centre forward was then brought down in front of goal and won a penalty. But centre half Charlie Hurley put the spot-kick wide of the right-hand post. If that was seen as a sign of the bad luck Sunderland would face in this match, it was confirmed shortly afterwards when Clough was unable to continue following a sickening collision in the twenty-seventh minute.

Chasing a loose ball in the hope it could lead to a goal, Clough collided with Chris Harker, his right knee crunching into the goalkeeper's shoulder. Clough was slightly off-balance, with his head down, as he concentrated on reaching the ball in the icy mud in the corner of the penalty area at the Fulwell End of Roker Park. Sunderland's Harry Hooper, who was not playing that day, said he could hear the impact of the collision even though he was sitting in the stand. Clough's head hit the ground and he said that for a moment all he could see was 'blackness'. But then he spotted that the ball was still loose and he tried in vain to get to his feet and reach it – film footage shows him crawl in agony. Later he recalled how centre half Stokoe apparently moaned at the referee. But the official, Kevin Howley from Clough's hometown of Middlesbrough, realised the seriousness of the situation. Sunderland's physiotherapist Johnny Watters came onto the pitch. It was soon clear there was little he could do at that point and the team was reduced to ten men as Clough was put on a stretcher and carried off. He was taken to hospital where the full extent of his injury became clear. Clough had damaged the cruciate ligament in his knee. It was the type of injury that could be overcome these days due to advances in medical treatment. But it meant his right leg was put in plaster, from the ankle to the thigh.

Back on the pitch, Bury scored the only goal of the game when a partial clearance by Ashurst reached Turner whose 25-yard drive went inside the left-hand post. But in the words of the *Sunderland Echo*'s report, defeat was only 'a minor tragedy' compared with the loss of their star centre forward, who was enjoying 'the brightest season of an already brilliant career'. Quoted years later in the *Northern Echo* newspaper, Chris Harker recalled the incident that led to the injury. He said, 'Brian went in for the ball with all his might. There were no hard feelings. There was snow and ice on the pitch. It was fifty-fifty and Brian just went over the top of me.'

Referring to how the injury eventually led to an outstanding managerial career for Clough, Harker continued, 'Whenever I watched him on TV after that, I used to think, "I'm the man who launched his career." Normally, I'm not even named, I am simply the "Bury goalkeeper", but what he did as a manager was amazing and I played a small part.'

Division One
Sunderland 2 West Bromwich Albion 2
2 September 1964

The finest goalscorer in the country and one of the best the game has ever seen, was no more.

It was to be a lengthy rehabilitation process for Clough following his cruciate ligament injury. Showing all the determination he had demonstrated as a top goalscorer in Division Two, the centre forward was focused on restoring his place in the Sunderland first team, which, in his absence, won promotion to the top tier in 1964. The rehab work included repeatedly running up and down the steps of the Kop at Roker Park to try to build up the strength in his injured knee. But secretly manager Alan Brown knew it was highly unlikely Clough would ever be the same player again – Brown wanted him to find out for himself, so there would be no doubt in Clough's mind. Sometimes Brown would join Clough in the challenging runs up and down the steep steps of the Roker Park terraces.

Eventually Clough made a return to first team action, more than eighteen months after suffering the shattering knee injury. It was the fourth League game of the season and fans were still eager to see Sunderland's first win following their return to the top flight of English football. In the first three matches they had drawn one and lost two. Supporters hoped that Clough's return in a midweek game against West Bromwich Albion would inspire a victory. A week earlier, they had been beaten 4-1 away by the same opposition.

Sunderland: McLaughlan, Irwin, Ashurst, Harvey, Hurley, McNab, Usher, Mitchinson, Clough, Crossan, Mulhall.
West Bromwich Albion: Potter, Cram, Williams, Fraser, Jones, Simpson, Foggo, Brown, Kaye, Hope, Clark.

Attendance: 52,177

It was almost a goalscoring return for Clough in a match described by *Sunderland Echo* football correspondent Argus as a 'thrill a minute' draw. In the first half, Clough saw his shot hit the post. He also came close near the end of the game, latching onto a great through ball from Tommy Mitchinson and hitting it towards the left of the goal. Unfortunately, the ball swerved inches wide of the post. The huge crowd was said to have been kept on its toes by the excitement and a Clough winner would have crowned what was described by Argus as 'an encouraging comeback' for him. Yet the match had started badly for the home side. The first touch of the ball for Sunderland's new goalkeeper Sandy McLaughlan was to pick it out of the net, after Brown scored with a header in the opening minute. Both Sunderland goals were equalisers. George Mulhall scored in the eleventh minute after hitting the ball through a crowd of players following a corner. Charlie Hurley, who was said to be playing in peak form, made it 2-2 in the second half with a header from a free-kick by Brian Usher. Although Sunderland had failed to secure their first win back in Division One, the report in the *Sunderland Echo* said they were making the right kind of progress and that a victory would not have been undeserved. Argus wrote that Clough still carried much of his former 'dash and fire', even though – as a perfectionist – he would have been frustrated with himself. It had been difficult for him to get into the game after a great first half, but his positional play was still impressive.

Three days later, on 5 September 1964, Clough retained his place in the side and scored what was to be his only goal in Division One. It came in a 3-3 draw at home to Leeds United, whose player-manager Don Revie was at right half. The rivalry between Clough and Revie, a former Sunderland captain, would increase intensely in the years to come. Playing in the second game of his long-awaited comeback, Clough was involved in a number of the early attacks. He had a header well saved by Humphreys before scoring in the seventh minute. Clough gave Humphreys no chance from 10 yards out. It was to be the last goal of an outstanding career as a centre forward. Struggling with the effects of his injury and sadly unable to find the same kind of goalscoring form he had shown in previous years, his final match for Sunderland was at home to Aston Villa on 9 September 1964 in front of a crowd of around 44,000. His name was not on the scoresheet in a 2-2 draw. His goalscoring record for Sunderland ended with fifty-four from sixty-one games. The curtain had come down on a playing career that produced an amazing 251 League goals in 274 appearances.

Clough was deeply apprehensive about what the future would hold; he had lived for scoring goals. But now that precious skill, which had brought so much pleasure to the Sunderland faithful, had been cruelly taken away. At the age of just twenty-nine he needed to discover a new lease of life. He found it by passing on his experience to young players. Sunderland's manager Alan Brown left to manage Sheffield Wednesday and his replacement, George Hardwick, gave Clough the opportunity to coach the club's youth team. It was a challenge he relished and carried out with great effect. The young players responded to his guidance positively as his flair for man-management began to blossom. He scrapped monotonous sessions of running laps of the pitch and instead encouraged them to practise playing with the ball, in the way they would on matchdays. Such was Clough's popularity that his testimonial match at Roker Park attracted a crowd of more than 30,000. With a young family and an uncertain future, he had the comfort of knowing that the receipts from the match (around £10,000) gave him some financial security. He never forgot the generosity of those Sunderland supporters. In the programme for Clough's testimonial match, Hardwick paid tribute to a man he admired both on and off the field, even though they had often clashed about their opinions of the way centre forwards should play. Hardwick wrote, 'The unfortunate accident that ended his career was, in my opinion, the saddest blow that England football has suffered, for I feel that the later years of his distinguished but short career would have been his greatest.'

The testimonial match programme also included a number of tributes from leading journalists of the time. Doug Weatherall of the *Daily Mail* said Clough was the greatest centre forward he had seen, while Bob Wood of the *News of the World* described him as the consistent goalscorer in English football since the war. Vince Wilson of the *Sunday Mirror* wrote, 'You could praise him, you could slam him – but you could never ignore Brian Clough. The club, the fans, the game and the sporting Press are the poorer for his absence.'

Hardwick did not last long in the manager's job and, following his departure, Clough was forced to look elsewhere too. The sun had set on his goalscoring career and although there had been a glimpse of autumn sunshine as he tried in vain to make a comeback, a new dawn was about to break as he was offered his first taste of management.

Division Four
Bradford City 1 Hartlepools United 3
30 October 1965

It won't be a little place for very long.

When Brian Clough was welcomed as the new manager of Hartlepools on 29 October 1965, no one could have predicted the huge impact the former centre forward would have on the world of football management. Clough used the humble beginnings on the north-east coast as a fantastic grounding for what would become, in many people's opinion, the greatest managerial career in the sport. 'Hartlepools won't be at the bottom of the Fourth Division for very much longer,' he told guests at his testimonial dinner at Sunderland, just a few days before he started the new job. In the outspoken style that would become so familiar in the years to come, he added, 'If you want to see some good stuff from Saturday onwards, get yourself down to a little place called Hartlepools. It won't be a little place for very long.'

Clough had been recommended for the job at Hartlepools (the 's' was later dropped when the two boroughs were united) by the former Sunderland player Len Shackleton, who wrote a well-respected column in a national newspaper. But a week before Clough's appointment was confirmed, he was one of three names being linked with the job. The others were the ex-Sunderland manager George Hardwick and Len Richley, a former Hartlepools player who had been boss at Kings Lynn. Following Clough's testimonial match, and a home defeat for Hartlepools at the hands of Barnsley, it was confirmed that the former Middlesbrough and Sunderland centre forward had been appointed on a two-year contract, earning £2,500 a year; it made him one of the highest paid managers in the Fourth Division. At the age of thirty he was the youngest manager in the Football League. The Hartlepools chairman, Ernie Ord, said he was delighted: 'I am very pleased that we have secured his services and I feel sure he is going to do a good job here,' he said. 'I am confident that we will soon be moving up the table.' Clough admitted that he had thought about the job carefully before accepting it. He said he and the club had talked for a week before reaching an agreement.

Hartlepools had gained a reputation for being the whipping boys of the basement division. In later years, Clough joked that – before he joined – the club must have set a world record for the number of times they had sought re-election to the Football League because they finished bottom. 'We were the scrubbing rags of the scrubbing rags,' he said. Nevertheless, the club was the ideal place for a young and ambitious manager to learn his trade. The challenges he faced, including limited resources, a difficult chairman and boosting the confidence and performance of some average players, certainly stood him in good stead for the rest of his career. In many ways, his approach to management at Victoria Park became a blueprint for how he would tackle the job at places like Brighton, Derby and Nottingham Forest in the future. In a television interview, filmed in black and white as he started his management career, his confidence and self-belief were clear for all to see. 'The things that are hard work to other managers are not hard work to me,' he said. 'The discipline side of it, the judging of players, the training, the coaching – these are not problems as far as I am concerned.' Before his first match as Hartlepools manager, against Bradford City, he was asked about his plan of action. 'I am aiming to win on Saturday and win the following Saturday,' he replied. 'Then you can come back and ask me the same question, and you will get the same answer.' He insisted that there was a place at the club for every player who gave 100 per cent effort.

Bradford City: Wood, Ingle, I. Cooper, Stowell, Fox, Smith, Hall, Hannah, Donnelly, Ellam, Thorpe. Sub: Rodon.
Hartlepools: Simpkins, Marshall, Drysdale, Fogarty, Harrison, Ashworth, J. Cooper, Wright, Phythian, McPheat, Mulvaney. Sub: Brass.

Attendance: 2,373

On a muddy pitch at Valley Parade, Hartlepools welcomed their new boss with a win against the side at the bottom of Division Four. Although the visitors had to defend for much of the first twenty minutes, Cliff Wright gave them the lead after twenty-one minutes with a close-range shot. He had brought the ball down after receiving it from a Jimmy Mulvaney free-kick and slotted it into the corner of the net from 10 yards. It was only Hartlepools' second League goal of the season away from home. They went 2-0 ahead in the thirty-fifth minute when a shot from Barry Ashworth was punched away by goalkeeper Ray Wood as far as Mulvaney, who scored from a tight angle. But Bradford responded quickly and made it 2-1 at half-time. Roy Ellam hit a half volley high into the net. The greasy surface of the pitch caused problems for both teams, with the ball either sticking in patches of water or fizzing across the wet grass. Hartlepools made certain of the two points when they scored a third goal six minutes from time. It was Mulvaney's second of the match after enterprising play from centre forward Ernie Phythian, who accelerated past three players to set up the goalscoring opportunity. The football correspondent of the *Hartlepool Mail*, Sentinal, described United as playing with a new spirit, showing both fight and endeavour – qualities which had been lacking up until now. He wrote, 'Pools' win must be viewed with a full recognition of Bradford's shortcomings, but nevertheless an away win, whatever the opposition, is an achievement.'

In his regular column in the newspaper's football edition that Saturday, Sentinal wrote that Clough's appointment, on paper, was an inspired answer to the team's predicament. A side whose basic problem was an inability to score goals now had a manager whose expertise had been finding the back of the net time after time. Unfortunately, the solution was not that simple, added Sentinal, who had written the column before the Bradford game. The article made it clear that if he did not know it already, Clough would realise there were many challenges to face. The columnist added,

He has certainly inherited one of the most difficult tasks in the Football League at the moment: he is to assume control of a struggling team, with a deplorable record over the past six seasons, and which, at the moment, shows no sign of improving it. He will have, apparently, little money to spend on improvements, and may well have to juggle and experiment with the material he has.

It was exactly the type of challenge Clough relished. He rolled up his sleeves, came up with a plan and made an important phone call to his football soulmate.

Division Four
Hartlepools United 4 Crewe Alexandra 1
6 November 1965

To describe Hartlepools' ground as a tip would be giving a bonus to a tip.

The television cameras arrived at the Victoria Ground for Brian Clough's first home match as Hartlepools manager. The highlights of the game were shown on the Tyne Tees television programme *Shoot!* following an edition of *The Avengers* called 'The Master Minds'. The latter title turned into quite a fitting description of what was to develop at the football club, as Clough had now been joined by his friend and former Middlesbrough teammate Peter Taylor. Together they would begin to mastermind the transformation of a lowly, struggling club with a dilapidated ground and lay the foundations for a much brighter future. Clough had approached Taylor, then manager at non-League Burton Albion, and they met at a hotel in York to discuss the prospect of working together. The former goalkeeper accepted Clough's offer to join him, taking on the official title of 'coach' or 'trainer' as the club was sceptical about the need for a manager to have an official 'assistant' in those days. It marked the start of an amazing managerial partnership.

Taylor arrived at the Victoria Ground on the Thursday before the match against Crewe and spent time speaking to club officials and meeting the players before heading back to Burton for a game that evening. The Southern League club had been enjoying a successful run in Division One and was challenging for promotion to the Premier Division. Burton agreed to release Taylor from his contract. 'You may ask why a manager of a successful non-league club joins a struggling league side as assistant manager,' Taylor told the local press. 'The answer is that I want success and I know that under Brian Clough we will achieve that success. We were close friends at Middlesbrough and I quickly learned to respect him both as a man and as a professional.' Clough said he was delighted that Taylor was joining the club. 'He knows the game as well as anyone,' he said, 'and I am more than glad to have him here working with me.' Taylor returned to Hartlepools for the match on Saturday.

Hartlepools United: Simpkins, Marshall, Drysdale, Fogarty, Harrison, Brass, Cooper, Wright, Phythian, McPheat, Mulvaney. Sub: Hamilton.
Crewe Alexandra: Mailey, Marshall, Leigh, Jones, Stott, Bodell, Walton, Matthews, Kane, Wheatley, Bradshaw. Sub: Gannon.

Attendance: 4,302

Hartlepools were forced to make one change to the team that had beaten Bradford City the previous week. Barry Ashworth had to serve a two-week suspension, meaning there was a place for part-timer Bobby Brass. He was making his first League start of the season, having been brought on as a substitute earlier in the month. Hughie Hamilton was drafted in as substitute this time. The visitors nearly went ahead after just six minutes when a Graham Matthews shot hit the bar and Ken Simpkins was able to grab the ball on the line. At the other end, Ernie Phythian went close with a shot that hit the goalkeeper's legs four minutes later. Phythian was caught offside on two occasions but he got his revenge in the fifteenth minute by putting Hartlepools ahead with a close-range shot. An impressive overhead kick by Cliff Wright made it 2-0 just after half an hour.

Phythian caused all kinds of problems for the Crewe defence and had the ball in the net early in the second half, but the referee had already blown for a foul against Mulvaney. Crewe reduced the deficit thanks to a goal from Peter Kane after sixty-five minutes, but the home side restored their two-goal advantage two minutes later with another goal by Phythian. He could have had a hat-trick but, for the second time in the match, his shot hit the goalkeeper's legs. With two minutes left, Phythian intercepted a back-pass by Leigh and chipped the ball to Wright, who headed it home despite the efforts of a Crewe defender on the goal line. After that fourth goal, the pitch was invaded by young fans celebrating an impressive performance.

The win was significant because it lifted Hartlepools out of the bottom four. They were the only side in the bottom nine to win, leaving them fifth from bottom. Cynics were reported to have emphasised that Hartlepools had simply beaten two sides who were now below them. But in his column in Monday's *Northern Daily Mail*, Sentinal said there were obvious improvements to the team's early season play. The attack had speed and power while the no-nonsense defence was looking more solid. Centre half Harrison was praised for his tight marking and 'no frills' approach to the job of clearing the ball and minimising any danger. Sentinal's verdict was that Hartlepools had been 'full value' for a win that promised much for the following week's FA Cup tie against Workington.

14

FA Cup: First Round
Hartlepools United 3 Workington 1
13 November 1965

The job we have to do will take time and patience, but I am confident we can do it.

The local newspaper described this FA Cup tie as the biggest test for Hartlepools since Brian Clough had taken over as manager. Workington were challenging for the top of Division Three and were said to be playing with 'lashings of confidence'. Fortunately, Clough had the same quality in bucketloads too and it was to rub off onto the players. According to a newspaper report, they underwent some intense pre-match-planning sessions under Clough's man-management expertise. The day before the game, he stressed how he wanted goals from his forward Willie McPheat. The forward duly obliged with his first two for the senior team in this excellent victory. It was clear that Clough was looking for a positive approach to the game. 'If you are depressed or low in spirit, you do not do the things in your work that you would normally do,' he said. 'If you're a footballer it means that you don't run, that there's no effort on the field. We have now overcome this and we have been helped by the start we have had, and there is no doubt the players are pulling very hard for me.' He also tried to manage the expectation levels of supporters. 'I know we will get better,' he said, 'but we are not going to beat everything right away. The job we have to do will take time and patience, but I am confident we can do it.'

In the run-up to the match, the Hartlepools players had been given a break from their routine by having a workout on Middleton Beach. It was under the guidance of the newly recruited physical training instructor Bryan Slater. He had joined the club from Burton Albion, where Peter Taylor had been manager. The players were said to be training harder than ever before, with a heavy emphasis placed on speed. Workington manager George Ainsley had watched Hartlepools' victory over Crewe the previous week and was reported to be impressed by their performance. Clough made one change to his line-up, bringing in defender Stan Storton after his two-week suspension.

Hartlepools: Simpkins, Storton, Drysdale, Fogarty, Harrison, Brass, Cooper, Wright, Phythian, McPheat, Mulvaney. Sub: Hamilton.
Workington: Ower, Lumsden, Chapman, Hale, Brown, Middlemass, Lowes, Butler, Oliver, Moran, Foley.

Attendance: 7,466

Hartlepools had their first shot at goal after five minutes. The effort by McPheat was easily collected by Ower. Workington took the lead three minutes later when slack marking in the home side's defence allowed winger Lowes to cut inside and hammer the ball into the net. Hartlepools equalised in the sixteenth minute. Middlemass tried to get the ball back to Ower and McPheat intercepted, beat the goalkeeper and scored from close range. Hartlepools suffered a setback when Jimmy Cooper began limping and for twenty minutes before half-time he was unable to make any meaningful contribution. A great save by Simpkins from a Moran effort kept the score level at the break.

Lowes had been a big threat for the visitors during the first half and Drysdale had struggled to control him at times, but in the second half Mulvaney was helping to reduce the threat with some good covering work down Workington's right flank. Hartlepools began to gain the upper hand and took the lead through Bobby Brass on fifty-seven minutes. Ower had punched the ball out following a Mulvaney cross and Brass hit the ball first time from 25 yards. Eight minutes later, McPheat got his second, shooting from the edge of the penalty area after good build-up play. It prompted a pitch invasion by young fans celebrating a memorable victory.

A reader's letter in the *Northern Daily Mail* reflected a new-found optimism among some Hartlepools supporters. It also had a prophetic reference to a Clough nickname that would become well known many years later, Old Big 'Ead. The letter, from 'Groundsman', said,

I thought when I read Brian Clough's comments on being appointed 'Pools manager that he was either talking with his tongue in his cheek, or that he had the 'biggest head' in football. Now the side I've watched through thick and thin (though mostly thin) seems to have a new urgency, and that essential will to win. If the present bubble does not burst, I shall be the first to take back all my cynical thoughts about the 'Clough Saga'. And even if 'Pools should fade again, they will have at least my continuing support.

While the Hartlepools first team enjoyed victory over Workington, new signing Tony Parry was making his debut in a defeat for the reserves at York. The nineteen-year-old inside forward was Clough's first signing and joined from Peter Taylor's former club, Burton Albion. He was described by the local newspaper as showing 'the speed, ball control and tenacity to be a big hit at the Victoria Ground'. The win in the FA Cup was rewarded with a home tie against struggling Wrexham, who were near the bottom of Division Four. Clough's immediate reaction to the draw was, 'I'm over the moon. Any home draw is a good draw.' He was asked whether he felt confident about the result. 'I'm never confident until the ninety minutes are over,' he replied, 'but if the team can maintain the effort they have given so far, we cannot go far wrong. We shall certainly be working very hard to achieve success.'

The players had a training session on Seaton Carew beach in preparation for the Wrexham match, which they won 2-0 with goals from Wright and Mulvaney. Decades later, Clough reflected on how bitterly cold it was when training on the coast. 'I'll give you a tip,' he told a Tyne Tees television documentary, 'never go training on a winter's day on Seaton Carew beach. It is the coldest place you have ever been in your life when the wind's blowing off the sea. I'm telling you, it's that cold you had to keep running to keep your circulation going.' He also had a dig at some of the overseas players who had arrived in the north-east and struggled to cope with the cold weather. He said,

> It makes me laugh when I read newspaper stories now about the foreigners who've gone to play at Middlesbrough and some get fed up after about six months and they put out the excuse that the wives can't get used to the climate. Now I assume when they first come to Middlesbrough they don't expect bl**dy palm trees – because I lived there thirty-odd years and I never saw a palm tree. There's certainly no bl**dy coconuts. The nearest we came to a coconut was when I used to go conkering.

The victory over Wrexham meant Hartlepools were now in the third-round draw with the big boys. Unfortunately, they were not rewarded with the plum tie they had hoped for. They travelled to Division Two side Huddersfield Town and lost 3-1 in front of more than 24,000 spectators. In the League, hard reality began to bite after the initial victories under Clough. The club went seven games without a win, including a 6-1 defeat at Tranmere on New Year's Day 1966. But then progress was made, with the help of new signings. Clough introduced a regional scouting system in which the scouts were paid by results. He tackled the defensive shortcomings with new additions like the no-nonsense defender John Gill from Mansfield, Brian Grant from Nottingham Forest and goalkeeper Les

Green from Burton. When Clough died in 2004, Grant paid tribute to his former boss, telling the *Cambridge News* that he was a fabulous man and highlighting his tremendous man-management skills even in those early days. 'There were times when he would give you the biggest rollicking of your life but when you sat down you realised you deserved it,' said Grant. 'Another day he would know something had happened at home and it would be an arm round the shoulder. He knew when to shout and when to comfort.'

The importance of a courageous defence had been instilled in Clough by another mentor (in addition to Sunderland boss Alan Brown), Harry Storer, who had managed Coventry and was introduced to Clough by Peter Taylor. Storer had told the impressionable young Clough that if he ever became a manager he should always have a good look at his players on the team coach before leaving for an away match. If he could count five hearts among them, he was lucky. If there were not that many, they should turn around and go back. It was advice Clough would remember throughout his managerial career.

Hartlepools were bottom of the League before a home victory over fellow strugglers Aldershot in February gave them hope. The line-up for that match was as follows: Green, Grant, Drysdale, Ashworth, Gill, Storton, Wright, Thompson, Phythian, Fogarty and Bradley. The goals in an easy 3-0 win came from Ernie Phythian, Ambrose Fogarty and Peter Thompson. There was a further boost when the side took the maximum six points from three matches over the Easter period, beating Stockport twice (2-1, both at home and away) and Notts County 2-0. Only four other clubs in the entire Football League had achieved a 100 per cent record over that holiday period. 'The results speak for themselves, but I am more delighted with the way we got them rather than the fact that we won,' said Clough. 'Once again it was spirit and fight from the players which did it.' He had decided against keeping the same line-up for all three games, showing that he was willing to change tactics as well as personnel to address different situations. At last Hartlepools were now out of the bottom four. With further wins over Chester, Lincoln City and Barrow, Hartlepools finished the season in eighteenth place. The final match of the League campaign, a 1-1 draw at home to Bradford City, saw the debut of sixteen-year-old John McGovern, who would later follow Clough to Derby, Leeds and Nottingham Forest, twice lifting the European Cup as the Forest captain.

Division Four
Brentford 1 Hartlepools United 2
27 December 1966

If everyone had increased their rate of productivity as much as my players, the country wouldn't be in the financial mess it's in now.

Brian Clough started his first full season in charge of a football club shortly after England had won the World Cup. He had spent the close season trying to improve Hartlepools' dilapidated ground. The situation had become so bad that buckets were needed to collect the water leaking through the roof of the boardroom and in the stands. In an effort to spruce things up, Clough and Taylor helped with painting work. As well as a paintbrush, Clough took tackling the club's financial plight into his own hands by visiting social clubs and businesses in order to attract investment. One of his rousing visits resulted in a Christmas present from the Rift House Social Club, which agreed to give the football club £120 in six monthly instalments – the money was for new roofing in the ground's Rink End stand. Clough described the donation as fantastic. 'And I mean it,' he said, 'I simply went in, talked to the committee for fifteen minutes, they discussed what I had said, and within ten minutes offered us £120.' The club had originally appealed for volunteers to come forward to fit a new roof. 'Some people came forward but it would have taken us till next April to finish it,' said Clough. Other social clubs also promised help, with one buying £100 worth of season tickets to distribute to its members. Clough told the local newspaper that these clubs were helping Hartlepools United to its feet and the football club would do all it could to repay them where it mattered: on the pitch.

The *Northern Daily Mail* reported on Christmas Eve 1966 that the young manager was devoting so much time to the club that his wife Barbara claimed she was going to write a book called *Thank Goodness for Away Games*. Her argument, said the article, was that when Brian travelled with the team there were no worries – she knew that he would, at least, eat regularly and be home on time. When he was at home he was so busy that he disappeared in the morning and did not return until late at night, 'just in time to take in the epilogue on TV', said the report. In the space of five days he had seen his two young sons,

Simon and Nigel, for a total of an hour. He was travelling many miles to attend speaking engagements in order to raise money and he admitted 'I'll have to get my priorities right, it's stupid to go on like this. It's not fair to my wife and children.' In addition to using his persuasive powers to boost the club's coffers, Clough showed he was a master of public relations by having his photograph taken at the wheel of the team coach after passing his public service vehicle test. The message was clear: he was even ready to drive the coach in order to save money. At one stage, Clough offered to forego his wages while the financial situation was sorted out. It was an offer declined by the club's board of directors. The manager was also determined not to sell the club's assets, including the young winger John McGovern, who had attracted the attention of several Division One clubs. His manager described him as probably the best winger in the north-east at that time, but emphasised that the player was not for sale.

On the pitch, Hartlepools had started the 1966/67 season with a 1-1 draw at Aldershot. The side included new signings John Sheridan, who was an experienced defender from Notts County, and talented winger Mick Somers, who had joined from Torquay United. The goal came from Joe Livingstone, who also scored in the next match, a 2-1 win over Wrexham, alongside Ernie Phythian. As Christmas approached, the return fixture against Aldershot resulted in a 3-2 win and there was growing optimism among fans. The local newspaper published a letter from 'a 'Pools fanatic' reflecting their hope for the future. It read, ''Pools are at long last in the top six and I would like to give Brian Clough a pat on the back for getting 'Pools up where they are. Let's hope 'Pools keep up and win promotion to the Third Division next season.'

The fixtures over the festive period featured two matches against Brentford, home and away. More than 8,000 expectant fans turned out on Boxing Day for the game at Victoria Park, which ended in a 2-2 draw. Hartlepools fought back strongly after being two goals down at half-time. Centre forward Ernie Phythian scored a penalty and set-up the second goal for Livingstone. The result of the return match the following day moved Hartlepools up to the heady heights of fourth in the division. If any game demonstrated the dramatic transformation in the club's fortunes achieved by Clough over the previous twelve months, it was this one. They had started the year in the bottom four, escaped re-election in May and were now rubbing shoulders with the leading teams.

Brentford: Phillips, MacKenzie, Jones, Higginson, Gelson, Thomson, Scott, Ross, Lawther, Bedford, Docherty.
Hartlepools: Green, Bircumshaw, Drysdale, Sheridan, Aston, Parry, McGovern, Livingstone, Phythian, Mulvaney, Wright.

Attendance: 5,775

Clough brought in new signing Stan Aston at centre half to bolster the defence for the game at Brentford. The twenty-five-year-old from Burton Albion was a last-minute addition and confirmed his decision to join Hartlepools the night before the match. He was introduced to his new teammates when he met the coach on its way down the M1. Clough told the *Northern Daily Mail*, 'This is the best piece of business, for myself and for the club, that I have done since coming here. He will be the best centre half in the Fourth Division by the end of the season.' Aston slotted in well straightaway, keeping a tight rein on Brentford's prolific scorer Brian Bedford. It was against the run of play that Brentford took the lead in the fifty-fourth minute. Green was unable to hold a blistering shot by Thomson and Docherty slotted the loose ball into the net. That spurred the visitors to fight even harder. They equalised in the seventy-sixth minute with a goal from Phythian, who scored the winner with just five minutes left. His second goal, a lovely low drive into the corner of the net, was his seventeenth of the season and put him at the top of the Division Four scoring charts (including cup matches). The margin of the victory could have been even greater had it not been for Brentford's teenage goalkeeper Gordon Phillips who made a string of good saves. The local newspaper's match report had particular praise for the performances of Wright, McGovern and Mulvaney. Clough joked that his players would soon be earning more than him, due to win bonuses. He said that if more people had increased their productivity rates, like his team had, the country would not be in a financial mess.

Despite the victory taking his team up to fourth in the table, Clough played down the chances of winning promotion, due to the number of matches remaining and a squad that showed a lack of strength in depth. 'It's no use kidding anyone and I don't intend to,' he said. 'One thing we have achieved though is a top four place at Christmas. Whatever happens, even if we lose the next ten matches, nobody can take that away from us.' Unfortunately, the team lost their next three matches, before a 1-0 victory over Bradford City halted the dip in form. Phythian continued his goalscoring exploits, netting in that match and the following game against Chester (a 3-2 home win in front of nearly 8,000 spectators).

The final home match of the League campaign was described by the local press as a 'Somer's Day' as goals from Mick Somers and Phythian gave Hartlepools a 2-0 win over Bradford Park Avenue. Many years later, Somers reflected on his time with Clough and said he felt privileged to have played for him. 'He really was something else. Even though he was new to management when I knew him, you could tell he had something special, and it was obvious Hartlepools was just a small stepping stone for him onto bigger things.' The winger also recalled that the young manager was a strict disciplinarian. Players would be in trouble if they stepped out of line. Even in those early days, Clough's man-management was second to none. Said Somers, 'I lived in digs with four other players and one of them was a lad who didn't always toe the line and used to like a drink. But Cloughie knew everything that went on, and he came up with a great way of stopping this lad from going out the night before matches. He'd come round to our house and go "Come with me, young man!" and he'd get him to spend the night babysitting for his children.'

With the help of new signings like Somers, Clough had created a winning mentality. In 1981 he reflected, 'What I always remember at Hartlepool was the pleasure we got from winning matches. Whenever we won an away match, we used to sing on the way home on the coach.' He admitted that he did not know whether he had enjoyed his time at the club, but it had taught him some harsh lessons that would stand him in good stead for the rest of his managerial career. The lessons included how to deal with difficult chairmen. He had stood his ground with United's chairman Ernie Ord, who was then replaced by Clough's friend John Curry. Clough always remembered the advice he had received from his mentor Harry Storer. 'Don't ever forget,' he said, 'directors never say thank you.' In his book *His Way*, Pat Murphy says the cult of the manager, which eventually saw the likes of Malcolm Allison, Tommy Docherty and Ron Atkinson firmly in the limelight, had its origins at Hartlepools United, thanks to Clough. 'The Hartlepools experience was the first step towards Clough the manager getting more attention than his players,' says Murphy.

Hartlepools missed out on promotion in the 1966/67 season, but finished an extremely creditable eighth. When compared to the final League positions in the seasons just before Clough's arrival, Hartlepools' transformation had been amazing to watch. In retirement, Clough joked that the team he had inherited at Victoria Park lacked talent to such an extent that the only thing the midfield could create was confusion among themselves. The club's Victoria Park ground had also been transformed, with leaking stands repaired and the installation of floodlights. Average attendances were up by almost 1,000 – quite an achievement at a Fourth Division club. There is no doubt that Clough, along with his assistant Taylor, had laid the foundations for promotion – which was secured the following season. But the managerial pair were not there to see it. They were building a new empire at Derby County.

16

League Cup: Third Round Replay
Derby County 3 Chelsea 1
2 October 1968

This was easily the best performance since I came to Derby.

Derby fans sensed that something special was just around the corner after Brian Clough's Second Division side beat Division One Chelsea in the League Cup. In its preview of the game, the *Derby Evening Telegraph* described it as the club's biggest match in recent years. The first leg at Stamford Bridge had been a goalless draw and there was huge anticipation among supporters at the Baseball Ground that a resurgent Rams, under the guidance of Clough and his assistant Peter Taylor, could cause an upset in the cup.

Clough and Taylor had arrived at Derby in June 1967 following the recommendation once again of the former England player Len Shackleton, whose national newspaper column ensured he was in contact with key figures in the game. Clough had replaced the former Rams player Tim Ward as manager but his first season in charge at the Baseball Ground saw Derby finish one place lower in the table than under Ward. Although progress may have seen slow at the time, the seeds were being sewn for what was to follow. Among the first signings were John O'Hare, Roy McFarland and Alan Hinton. O'Hare had been coached by Clough in the youth team at Sunderland and proved to be an impressive centre forward, whose strong build helped to shield the ball from frustrated defenders. McFarland was snatched from under the noses of Liverpool when Clough and Taylor went to the Tranmere youngster's house at night to secure his signature. Clough's powers of persuasion meant the deal was done there and then, while the nineteen-year-old was still wearing his pyjamas. McFarland became a Derby legend, being exceptionally quick, uncompromising and skilful with the ball at his feet. Hinton was signed from local rivals Nottingham Forest and proved to be a vital addition. He could play on either wing and was both a creator and scorer of great goals. The most significant new arrival, however, was Dave Mckay. The barrel-chested Scot was inspirational on and off the pitch in his new role as sweeper. Clough had travelled down to Tottenham's White Hart

Lane ground to meet Mckay and convinced him to sign for Derby, even though he was poised to join Hearts as assistant manager and Derby were languishing in eighteenth place in Division Two. In Mckay's autobiography *The Real Mackay* he recalled his meeting with Clough:

> It was a lovely summer's day and we sat down on the turf next to where the corner flag would have been. He looked fit and young in a neat suit, collar and tie, with his hair quiffed back almost in Teddy Boy style. He looked more like a trainee bank manager than a football manager. He was positively evangelical about Derby County.

Clough told Mackay how Derby was a sleeping giant and he described to him the talent of each individual player in the side. 'His enthusiasm was infectious and his confidence shocking,' said Mackay. By the end of the discussion, Mackay had agreed to join Derby. Clough later wrote about the sense of complete elation he felt during the return car journey north after completing such a crucial deal. He said the feeling of triumph was 'quite brilliant' and that he had not made a more effective signing in his entire managerial career. Mackay was to be the 'crowning glory' for the talented side being assembled at the Baseball Ground. Despite the signing of the legendary Mackay, things got off to a slow start as the new season began.

Two draws and two defeats gave the fans little to cheer at the start of the 1968/69 season, but the signing of tenacious midfielder Willie Carlin from Sheffield United was to be a catalyst for a surge in form. Carlin made his debut in a 2-2 draw at home to Hull City at the end of August. That game marked the start of a fantastic run of twenty-two League matches with just one defeat. While fans were talking about the possibility of promotion, there was also excitement in the League Cup, which helped to increase the team's confidence and momentum. A 5-1 cup victory over Stockport County, which included four goals from Alan Hinton, led to the away tie against Chelsea. Derby did well to earn a replay against a strong side that included a number of internationals. The scene was set for a midweek battle at the Baseball Ground in front of more than 34,000 fans. In his book *Right Place Right Time*, the former *Derby Evening Telegraph* Rams reporter and sports editor George Edwards described the match as one of those 'I was there' occasions. He said it was the most exciting and dramatic match he had ever seen.

Derby County: Green, Webster, Robson, Durban, McFarland, Mackay, Walker, Carlin, O'Hare, Hector, A. Hinton. Sub: Barker
Chelsea: Bonetti, M. Hinton, McCreadie, Hollins, Webb, Harris, Birchenall, Tambling, Osgood, Hutchinson, Houseman. Sub: Lloyd

Attendance: 34,346

Clough replaced Richie Barker with the fit-again John O'Hare, despite Barker having scored in the previous league match, a 2-1 win at Bolton. Chelsea called-up twenty-year-old Ian Hutchinson to lead their attack. The local press predicted a 'fairy-tale debut' for Hutchinson, who was originally from Derby and had played for International Combustion in the Derby and District Senior League. Unfortunately for him, it was not quite the dream debut he would have wanted. Chelsea were described as 'chasing shadows' due to Derby's slick passing as the ball skidded along the wet surface. It was against the run of play that Alan Birchenall gave Chelsea the lead in the twenty-sixth minute with a fine shot from 30 yards. Derby did not give up and three goals in the last fifteen minutes finished off a Chelsea side which George Edwards, in his match report, described as being like a boxer 'staggering around the ring, battered, bewildered, not knowing which way to turn and finally sinking to the floor'.

The Rams fans got behind the team and created a tremendous atmosphere, with chants of 'Derby, Derby' thundering around the ground. The home side launched a wave of attacks, with the imposing Mckay inspiring his side to victory. He hit an equaliser into the top corner after a lovely back-heel by Carlin. Derby took the lead in the eighty-third minute when Alan Durban headed home a cross from the left by Jimmy Walker. Four minutes later Kevin Hector made it three and the Baseball Ground erupted once again. After the game, Clough was full of praise for his team. 'I was delighted for the players,' he said. 'This was easily the best performance since I came to Derby.' The club's chairman, Sydney Bradley, also spoke in glowing terms. 'This was a night I shall remember as long as I live,' he said. 'What a wonderful display by the team and how wonderful our supporters were.' The president of the Football League, Len Shipman, was also impressed and said, 'This reminded me of the Derby of twenty years ago. A wonderful match.' The manager of Derby's next opponents in the league, Middlesbrough, had been watching the match. Stan Anderson said Derby were 'easily the best Second Division team I have seen this season'. Lifelong Derby fan Ron Stevenson was also among the spectators. 'This was such a memorable match,' he said. 'It was this result that made me think that something special was going to happen. From that moment we knew there was nothing that could stop us getting to the First Division.' Ron was especially impressed with the young McFarland. 'He was like a bird when he rose to head the ball. He was so elegant it was unbelievable.' Dave Mackay described the victory over Chelsea as a turning point in Derby's season. It was therefore no surprise when the Rams won promotion to Division One a few months later.

17

Division Two
Derby County 5 Bolton Wanderers 1
5 April 1969

Well, that's phase one completed.

Derby's promotion to Division One was secured following victory over Bolton Wanderers during the first weekend of April 1969. It meant the Rams were back in the top flight for the first time in sixteen years – and there were still four league matches to play before the end of the season. After victories away at Oxford United, Aston Villa and Fulham in the previous three matches, Derby faced a struggling Bolton side who put up little resistance at the Baseball Ground. The visitors, managed by the former England forward Nat Lofthouse, had conceded fourteen goals in losing their previous three matches and were hampered by injury and illness. The Rams were without nineteen-year-old midfielder John McGovern, who had injured his ankle in the Rams' previous match against Fulham. That game had ended 1-0, with substitute Frank Wignall scoring the only goal. Wignall, a former Nottingham Forest forward, was brought into the starting line-up against Bolton. He was a big striker but liked to travel light. The former *Derby Evening Telegraph* journalist George Edwards recalled in his book *Right Place Right Time* how there had been no sign of Wignall carrying a bag when the coach picked him up for his first overnight away trip with his new team. Edwards wrote,

'Where's your bag, Frank? We're stopping over,' shouted Cloughie from one of the card tables towards the back of the coach, whereupon Frank put his hand into the inside pocket of his jacket and produced a toothbrush, which he brandished flamboyantly to the huge amusement of his new teammates.

Wignall scored four goals in six matches as Derby aimed to finish the 1968/69 season in style.

Derby County: Green, Webster, Robson, Durban, McFarland, Mackay, Wignall, Carlin, O'Hare, Hector, Hinton. Sub: Walker.
Bolton Wanderers: Hopkinson, Cooper, Farrimond, Williams, Marsh, Rimmer, Phillips, Hill, Byrom, Greaves, Taylor. Sub: Hallows.

Attendance: 30,684

Goals from Wignall and Kevin Hector gave Derby a 2-0 half-time lead over Bolton. The strong wind made it difficult for the players to control the ball, but it helped Derby to take the lead. Hector's goal saw him latch onto a long kick from goalkeeper Les Green. The ball bounced on the edge of the visitors' penalty area before the Derby player slid it past Eddie Hopkinson to make it 1-0. Wignall had a header cleared off the line by Farrimond before the striker volleyed the ball home with the last kick of the half. A surprise goal for the visitors in the fifty-seventh minute sparked Derby into showing their impressive form. They won a string of corners that caused problems for the Bolton defence, as McFarland and Wignall rose higher than the opposition. Two goals in five minutes put the result beyond any doubt. O'Hare and Carlin got on the scoresheet before McFarland, on his twenty-first birthday, hammered the ball into the net four minutes from time. Shortly after the final whistle it was announced that Middlesbrough had lost at Chelsea, meaning Derby were promoted.

Behind the scenes, Brian Clough was photographed opening a bottle of champagne for the players to enjoy. George Edwards reported that Clough was 'strangely quiet as his players sang, joked and toasted each other in champagne'. It was clear that Clough regarded the result as a stepping stone to greater triumphs. The manager commented 'well, that's phase one completed'. Within half an hour of the game he was meeting the parents of two teenaged triallists. When asked about the prospects for the following season, Clough responded, 'We won't set 'em alight up there, but we might surprise a few people.' He said that while his team would not score many goals, he hoped they would not concede many. He added 'of course there are people who say we will come straight down. They are the same people who said we would be relegated when we only took three points out of the first ten this season'. Peter Taylor was away on a scouting mission and Clough said it was a pity his assistant was not there to share the moment.

Despite the confirmation that Derby would be playing in Division One the following season, Clough ensured there was no complacency among the players. As the local press highlighted the possibility of the Rams finishing as champions, Clough said simply 'first things first', before his unchanged team faced Sheffield United in their next match. Alan Durban scored a late winner against the Blades.

It was one of nine successive victories that completed a memorable season and Derby were crowned Division Two champions. Supporters were urged to arrive early for the final match, against Bristol City, because the players conducted a lap of honour before kick-off. In front of more than 31,000 fans at a sunlit Baseball Ground, Derby put on a footballing show described by the headline in the *Derby Evening Telegraph* as 'Exhibition Soccer'. Alan Durban, back from international duty, scored a first-half hat-trick in a 5-0 victory. Alan Hinton hit Derby's fourth with a terrific left-foot shot that flew into the corner of the net. He later had a penalty saved by City's goalkeeper Barry Watling, who was deputising for Derby-born Mike Gibson. Hector headed in the fifth from a Hinton corner. Thousands of fans ran onto the pitch after the final whistle and, in the directors' box, the Division Two trophy was officially presented to Dave Mackay. He told the crowd, 'It will be a great pleasure to come back and win the First Division championship.' A newspaper report described Clough as being moved to tears as the crowd chanted and swayed on the pitch. He held the microphone and told the fans, 'Be careful of the pitch – we don't want to spoil our lovely pitch.' He then added, 'When anybody asks who did it, these lads did it.'

The result against Bristol City set a club record of twenty-six victories in a forty-two-match programme. It also sparked huge celebrations among fans in Derby's pubs that night. Even when a gang tried to take advantage of thousands of revellers by distributing forged £5 notes in the town centre, it failed to dampen the high spirits. At around midnight, crowds of supporters were still singing and chanting outside the Midland Hotel where the Rams were holding a celebration dinner. Speaking at the event, Clough paid tribute to Peter Taylor and each of the players. Describing Dave Mackay as inspirational, Clough said, 'Some people are said to be born with a silver spoon in their mouth, but he was born with a trophy in his hands.' Mackay told the gathering that it had been the finest season of his career and he hoped that the following campaign would be even better. Mackay had topped a fine season by being named Footballer of the Year, an award he shared with Manchester City's Tony Book. The future was looking bright for the Rams, who received a surge in ticket enquiries for their return to the top flight, especially after the announcement of a new stand across the Popular Side of the ground.

18

Division One
Derby County 2 Everton 1
6 September 1969

If we could play like this every week nobody would beat us, but we can't.

Derby began life back in the First Division by staying unbeaten in the seven matches they played during August 1969. The games included two victories, home and away, against Ipswich and a win at West Bromwich Albion. After beating his former club Hartlepool in the League Cup at the start of September, Clough was faced with what the local press described as Derby's first major battle of the season: a huge match at home to league leaders Everton. The visitors were unbeaten so far that season and had dropped only one point on their way to the top. On the day of the game, the *Derby Evening Telegraph* reported that the Derby players had been subjected to Clough's particular style of psychology and had been gathered together since the previous Thursday evening. They were, said Clough, 'physically and mentally prepared' for the match. He admitted he had not watched Everton ('because it might depress me') and he pinpointed the battle in midfield as the one that would dictate the course of the game. 'Players can rise to the occasion and I hope our lads will do this,' he said. 'The crowd can help by getting right behind us from the start. Everton are a very fine side and we do not underestimate them, but we are playing well and we must remember that they are not supermen.' Everton's right half Howard Kendall, who had been out of the team since the first day of the season with a leg injury, returned to the starting line-up.

Derby: Green, Webster, Robson, Durban, McFarland, Mackay, McGovern, Carlin, O'Hare, Hector, Hinton. Sub: Wignall.
Everton: West, Wright, Brown, Kendall, Labone, Harvey, Husband, Ball, Royle, Hurst, Morrissey. Sub: Jackson.

Attendance: 37,708

Many fans arrived early for the game, with the Baseball Ground at least half full an hour before the start. Everton kicked-off towards the Normanton end but the Rams soon gained possession, only for the England international Alan Ball to trip young John McGovern. That was the start of things to come. McGovern had become a first-team regular since the start of the year, after previously working with Clough at Hartlepool, and had signed a new contract during the summer. His brilliant man-marking of Ball was one of the highlights of the game. George Edwards, in his match report for the *Derby Evening Telegraph*, said McGovern shadowed Ball everywhere, leaving the England star in 'a state of frustration and near rage'. Willie Carlin took charge of midfield and, upfront, John O'Hare had centre halves Brian Labone and John Hurst arguing between themselves. In the thirty-ninth minute O'Hare got his reward and scored his first goal of the season to put Derby ahead. Everton's Gordon West could only punch out an Alan Hinton corner and O'Hare headed home from 6 yards out. The visitors also had chances and Les Green made a wonderful one-handed save from a close-range header by Hurst before half-time.

Everton put Derby under pressure early in the second half but the home side won a corner after a move involving eight of their players. From Hinton's corner in the sixty-seventh minute, Kevin Hector glanced the ball towards goal. Harvey headed it away but the referee confirmed the ball had crossed the line and Derby were 2-0 up. Everton attacked straightaway and within minutes they pulled a goal back. Derby failed to clear the ball from danger and Kendall's right-foot shot from the edge of the area went in off the far post. Carlin, who was described as the Man of the Match, won a free-kick that led to Derby almost scoring a third. From the set-piece Hector raced in for a superb header that West tipped over the bar. Everton put Derby's defence under some tremendous pressure towards the end of the game, but the Rams held out for an impressive victory to end the visitors' unbeaten run. The local newspaper said Derby had put a talented Everton side in a straitjacket. Clough was full of praise for his players and picked out O'Hare and McGovern for their contributions. 'The centre forward was out of this world,' he said. 'And John McGovern's ability to lay the ball anywhere first time with either foot is fabulous.' In his autobiography *From Bo'ness to the Bernabeu*, John McGovern said he had taken it upon himself to mark Ball and was not acting on specific orders. Clough waited for McGovern in the tunnel after the match and asked who had told him to mark Ball. When McGovern replied that nobody had told him and that he simply wanted to show Ball how well he could play, Clough's response was typically to the point, as McGovern explained,

'Well you did a great job for the side because he never got a kick,' said Brian. As I walked past him on my way to the dressing room, wallowing in the rare praise he had thrown my way, I got hit with the punchline. 'And he's a good player,' shouted Clough. 'You're not!'

McGovern said that despite the quip at the end, Clough's praise made him feel 'like a million dollars'. Speaking to the press, Clough would not make any predictions for the rest of the season. 'Only the great sides like Everton, Leeds and Liverpool can say for certain they will be up at the top next April,' he said. 'If we could play like this every week nobody would beat us, but we can't.' The Everton manager Harry Catterick was clearly not happy about his side losing their unbeaten run to a newly promoted team. Asked about Derby, he responded, 'They are just an ordinary side.' Over the following weeks and months, the Rams would continue to prove that simply was not the case.

19

Division One
Derby County 5 Tottenham Hotspur 0
20 September 1969

We must win for David's sake.

Brian Clough walked onto the Baseball Ground pitch to receive his Manager of the Month award, before this memorable match against Dave Mackay's former club. Clough was handed a cheque for £50 and a gallon bottle of whisky. In later years, Clough's continued success would see him become a regular recipient of the award. Derby had remained unbeaten during August 1969 and the momentum continued into September with wins over Everton, Southampton and Newcastle United. With Liverpool losing 1-0 at Manchester United, the Rams were now the only unbeaten side in Division One. The Liverpool manager, Bill Shankly, was obviously wary of Derby because he was in the stand to watch the 3-0 victory against Southampton. Clough's side had climbed to second in the table while Spurs had the best away record in the division and were fifth.

As the match drew closer, Clough emphasised its significance. 'We must win for David's sake,' he said, referring to Rams' skipper Mackay. Using the player's full name was a typical Cloughism; just ask Edward Sheringham, Desmond Walker and Kenneth Burns. For Clough, it would never be Teddy, Des or Kenny. He said the use of any kind of nickname would be a sign of over-friendliness between manager and player. In 1999, he told the BBC *Match of the Day* magazine,

> When I called young Sheringham 'Edward', people seemed to be very amused, but he told me that his parents did the same. Anyway, in Yorkshire, we like to use the proper first names – as Anthony Adams, Robert Moore and Terence Butcher would have found out if they'd ever played for me.

Clough's decision to remind people about the importance of winning the game against Mackay's former club only added to the fans' expectations. A record crowd of nearly 42,000 crammed into the ground to watch a special piece of history, as the man who had enjoyed such an incredible career at the London club – winning Division One and FA Cup winners medals – was now in a newly promoted side aiming to beat them. 'I had some great times with Spurs, but I play for Derby County now,' said Mackay before the game. 'I shall be the proudest man in England when I lead the lads out.' Clough, too, was looking forward to the fixture. 'Tomorrow's game promises to be a good spectacle and I know our lads will be giving everything for David's sake,' said the manager. 'He wants to win this match more than anything'.

Derby County: Green, Webster, Robson, Durban, McFarland, Mackay, McGovern, Carlin, O'Hare, Hector, Hinton. Sub: Wignall.
Tottenham Hotspur: Jennings, Beal, Knowles, Mullery, England, Collins, Pearce, Greaves, Gilzean, Pratt, Morgan. Sub: Want.

Attendance: 41,826

Despite winning their previous four away matches, Spurs were reduced to 'an inept shambles', according to the *Derby Evening Telegraph*. George Edwards summed it up in his report on the game when he wrote, 'It wasn't a match; it was a massacre.' After twenty-five minutes, Spurs had been left stunned by three brilliant goals. Although the visitors were down to ten men for the last twenty minutes when Pratt limped off, the game was effectively over by then anyway. Derby took the lead in the fifteenth minute. The Welsh international Mike England, who was given a torrid afternoon by John O'Hare, tried to turn the ball back to goalkeeper Pat Jennings after finding himself under pressure down the right. But Alan Durban moved in quickly and hit a right-foot shot just inside the far post. Four minutes later, Derby were 2-0 up. O'Hare controlled a throw-in, turned away from England and pushed the ball through to Kevin Hector, who shrugged off a challenge and hit a tremendous shot into the Spurs net.

The visitors almost got a goal back but an outstanding save by Les Green denied England forward Jimmy Greaves. Mackay would later describe it as the best save he had ever seen by a goalkeeper and said it was even better than the save that England's Gordon Banks made from Pele's header in the 1970 World Cup in Mexico. Greaves unleashed a fierce volley from around 15 yards out and it seemed a certain goal. Mackay said the shot was so strong that he had expected the ball to rip the back of the net. Green dived to his left across the goal and not only stopped the shot, but also clutched the ball with both hands. Mackay leapt feet into the air as he watched. 'It was like someone firing a rifle in your direction and you effortlessly catching the bullet,' he said in his autobiography *The Real Mackay*.

The Derby skipper said his former team was 'pulversied'. The Rams were 3-0 up at half-time, with McFarland at his dominant best. Willie Carlin headed Derby's third after a corner from Alan Hinton. Carlin was also part of an impressive move that led to the fourth goal in the sixty-second minute. He weaved his way past three players on the right and turned the ball inside for Durban who nutmegged Beal and turned the ball back for O'Hare to hammer an unstoppable shot past Jennings. 'Once again it was almost cruelty to see Spurs ripped apart,' reported Edwards. Durban scored his second of the match with a header after sixty-eight minutes. Shortly afterwards, he was replaced by Frank Wignall due to a groin strain.

After the game, the Spurs manager Bill Nicholson said Derby had humiliated his team. 'They are very talented and they don't just run, they know when to run and where,' he said. He described Carlin as 'brilliant' and also had praise for John McGovern. 'One second he was tackling somebody in his own penalty area and the next he was having a shot at the other end.' Nicholson said Mackay was an inspiration and a credit to the game. Mackay himself said he was happy for his team. 'Not because it was Spurs we beat but because you can't be anything but happy when you are in a team which plays like that. It is the best we have played since I came here.'

Clough was unusually understated when asked for his assessment of the match. 'You don't need to say anything after that,' he said. 'I am just very happy for the lads. I was very proud of them.' He said he could not pick out a Man of the Match. 'The lads will all tell you that John O'Hare was and I suppose when you see a centre half [Mike England] stumbling about like a blind man, that's fair enough.' Referring to critics who regarded O'Hare as being too slow, Clough added, 'I think even the real idiots who don't understand football twigged John O'Hare this afternoon.'

The comprehensive victory over Spurs demonstrated that Derby could compete successfully at the highest level in domestic football. Further wins against Manchester United and Liverpool that season underlined the fact. New signing Terry Hennessey, who joined Derby from local rivals Nottingham Forest, scored in a 2-0 victory at Anfield. That match was part of a twelve game unbeaten run at the end of the 1969/70 season that saw the Rams finish fourth in their first season back in the top flight. A place in Europe was denied due to administrative irregularities, but it became a reality two seasons later when Derby won the League Championship for the first time.

20

Division One
Derby County 1 Liverpool 0
1 May 1972

You cannot imagine a better place to be when you're top of the League.

It was a warm night full of excitement and expectation for Derby fans. In the lead-up to this final match of the season, Brian Clough described it as the most important game since he and Peter Taylor had taken over at the Baseball Ground nearly five years earlier. The Rams needed to beat title rivals Liverpool in order to keep alive their hopes of winning the League Championship for the first time. The pressure was on. Even if Derby won, both Liverpool and Leeds had a further match to play after this one and would be able to leapfrog Clough's side.

The importance of the game was not lost on Liverpool's fans, with the *Derby Evening Telegraph* reporting that thousands of supporters from Merseyside had arrived in Derby by midday, many of them without tickets. Around 3,000 ticketless fans were locked outside the ground by the time the match kicked-off. The Liverpool manager, Bill Shankly, arrived at the ground before lunchtime. He said his team had stayed in Nottingham overnight and two coachloads of fans turned up there. They had just one ticket between them, he said. Shankly's side were full of confidence, having taken twenty-eight points out of a possible thirty in their previous fifteen games. While Clough had been pleased with Derby's 2-0 home win against Don Revie's Leeds United a month earlier, they had suffered a setback by losing 2-0 at Manchester City. As the crucial match against Liverpool approached, Clough said, 'I just hope it is a fine game and that our fans respond to the occasion and cheer us along just as they did against Leeds.'

The pre-match press reports indicated that Derby would include sixteen-year-old Steve Powell in their line-up. Although it was only Powell's second start in a league match, Clough had no hesitation in playing him at right-back instead of the injured Ron Webster. 'I don't consider his age, just his ability and temperament,' said the manager before the game. His decision was vindicated. Despite Liverpool's danger men such as Kevin Keegan, Steve Heighway and John Toshack, Derby produced a superb defensive display, with young Powell playing exceptionally well.

Derby County: Boulton, Powell, Robson, Durban, McFarland, Todd, McGovern, Gemmill, O'Hare, Hector, Hinton. Sub: Hennessey.
Liverpool: Clemence, Lawler, Lindsay, Smith, Lloyd, Hughes, Keegan, Hall, Heighway, Toshack, Callaghan. Sub: McLaughlin.

Attendance: 39,420

Two well-organised defences meant there were few clear-cut chances in the match. Colin Todd, who Clough had spotted when he was a youth coach at Sunderland, justified his choice by Derby supporters as their Player of the Year. Alongside him, Roy McFarland was dominant against Toshack. Derby's winning goal came in the sixty-third minute. Kevin Hector took a throw-in on the right and Archie Gemmill hit a low cross into the penalty area. Alan Durban allowed the ball to run through his legs and it came to John McGovern who thumped it into the top corner. McGovern lost his balance as he took the vital shot and has since explained that he was surprised that Durban had let the ball run to him. In his autobiography *From Bo'ness to the Bernabeu* he recalls,

> Alan Durban leaving a shooting opportunity to someone else was unheard of, so you could have literally knocked me down with a feather, which explains why I was off balance as the ball screamed into the net. Off balance or not, I knew my connection was fine. The eruption of noise from the crowd confirmed I had hit the target.

In the search for an equaliser, Liverpool took off Heighway and replaced him with McLaughlin after seventy-two minutes. The substitute forced Boulton to make a save and push the ball away, with Durban on hand to thump the ball to safety. The final whistle saw hundreds of fans run onto the pitch. Derby had secured a vital win and their young defender Powell was the focus for much of the praise afterwards. Bill Shankly made a point of shaking his hand and congratulated him on his performance. The youngster had shown maturity way beyond his years, at one stage cleverly controlling the ball and flicking it over the head of Emlyn Hughes. Lifelong Derby fan Ron Stevenson was at the match and told me he was hugely impressed by Powell. 'He had absolutely no fear, he was tackling some of the country's top players and it didn't bother him,' said Ron. 'You could see how talented he was. He didn't need any protection from the other players even though he was only sixteen. That win against Liverpool meant the title was within our grasp for the first time. We were within touching distance of greatness.' The championship now hinged on the final matches of the season. Liverpool needed to win at Arsenal, while Leeds, who had already won the FA Cup, required only a draw at Wolves to secure the double. Many of the Derby players joined Clough's assistant Peter Taylor for a sunshine break in Majorca while they waited to hear the results. The *Derby Evening Telegraph* reported that Steve Powell was staying behind to continue studying for his A-Level exams.

Clough took his family to the Scilly Isles while he waited for the results of the Liverpool and Leeds matches. Liverpool were held to a goalless draw by Arsenal at Highbury and Leeds lost 2-1 at Wolves. It meant the sixty-eight points that Derby had already amassed was enough to win the title. Leeds, Liverpool and Manchester City finished one point behind. Some of the national press concluded that Derby had won the championship by default. It was something that still annoyed Clough many years later. 'Twisted thinking,' he called it, saying you could not fluke a title over forty-two games. The local newspaper gave credit where it was due, stating that Derby had won the championship on merit by their consistent skill and hard work since August.

Speaking from the island of Tresco, Clough told the press, 'You cannot imagine a better place to be when you're top of the league. I'm just about to take my wife and bairns to see the flowers and the gardens.' He said he had never given up hope of winning the title. 'Talented players have won the league for us,' he added. 'It is obviously more of a feat for Derby to finish top than one of the big city clubs.' In his first autobiography, Clough said it had been nice that his parents were there with him on the Scilly Isles to share the moment. He recalled that the following days, after learning that Derby had won the most precious prize in football, were some of the happiest he could remember.

Although Liverpool had been pipped to the post, Bill Shankly was generous in his praise. He described Derby as worthy Champions and said that with their attacking flair they should do well in the European Cup. 'Brian Clough has built a great side,' said Shankly. 'His players are young and full of ability and to win a League Championship so soon after entering the First Division is a credit to his methods.' He said Derby were the best team his side had played during the season. 'I don't take anything away from Leeds when I say Derby are a better all-round team.' Forget the Beatles, those comments from Liverpool's legendary manager must have been sweet music to Clough's ears.

21

European Cup: First Round, First Leg
Derby County 2 FK Zeljeznicar 0
13 September 1972

It really grabbed you to watch such a display.

Brian Clough approached his first European Cup match with the confidence that characterised his career. 'We can win the European Cup,' he told the press ahead of Derby's first experience of the prestigious club competition. The Rams faced the champions of Yugoslavia, Zeljeznicar Sarajevo, who were reputed to be a physical team. On the night of this momentous game, television viewers were treated to the latest episode of *Mission: Impossible* on BBC1. But that was a phrase never within the vocabulary of the optimistic Clough. 'We have an excellent chance, both tonight and in the whole competition, because I think we have a skilful side at Derby,' he said. The team would need physical strength as well as skill, he added. 'We have played well away from home and come back with nothing to show for it. It's time we turned it on for our own crowd.'

Yet it seemed the prospect of European football had not caught the imagination of some of the Derby public. Even on the day of the match, there were still tickets available. To sit in the centre of the Ley Stand, fans were charged £1.50, while a ticket for the Osmaston Terrace was 60p. Speaking the day before the game, Clough said he hoped supporters would turn out in numbers to give their backing to the players at such a crucial time. 'Certainly I am not begging anybody to watch us but I do know that our players will need a full house tomorrow,' he said. While he accepted that the side had made a mediocre start to defending their League title, this game was the culmination of five years' hard work and forty-two matches in the previous season. Clough had a strong message for those who had said Derby were lucky to win the title and had felt justified in their opinion after the side's subsequent slow start. He declared that 'we will ram their words down their throats to such as extent that they will never treat us lightly again.'

Derby County: Boulton, Powell, Daniel, Hennessey, McFarland, Todd, McGovern, Gemmill, O'Hare, Hector, Hinton. No subs used.
Zeljeznicar Sarajevo: Janjus, D. Kojovic, Becirspahic, Derakovic, Katalinski, Bratic, Jelusic, Jankovic, Bucal, Spreco, Radovic. Subs used: S. Kojovic, Saracevic.

Attendance: 27,350

Derby drafted in Peter Daniel to take over in defence from David Nish, who was ineligible to play. 'And it goes without saying that he wouldn't be playing if we did not think he could make a great job of it,' said Clough. Sarajevo had brothers Dragan and Slobodan Kojovic in their squad. Nineteen-year-old Slobodan, a reserve-team striker, came on as a substitute at half-time; his twenty-one-year-old brother played at right-back. As the match progressed, the visitors were forced to defend for long periods. The *Derby Evening Telegraph* reported that a great team performance by the Rams reduced Zeljeznicar 'to tatters'. Derby's opening goal came in the thirty-ninth minute and was described as 'a curious affair'. Goalkeeper Janjus looked uncomfortable dealing with crosses and when Alan Hinton sent in a free-kick it was missed by the 'keeper. Roy McFarland headed towards goal and Spreco appeared to handle the ball as it was going in. While Derby appealed for a penalty, the referee awarded a goal because the ball had dropped over the line.

In midfield, Terry Hennessey was an impressive figure. Having signed from local rivals Nottingham Forest, he showed examples of his previous outstanding form. His tackling, passing and bursts of attacking-play were praised by the press and Clough after the game. 'He was absolutely superb and yet he could have been out of the side if Alan Durban had been fully fit,' said the manager. 'Terry will be even more essential to us when we travel to Sarajevo.' Archie Gemmill's pace was also a decisive factor in the game. Derby's second goal came from a shot by Gemmill that hit Janjus before it went into the net. The visitors' goal continued to be peppered and seemed to live a charmed life. A header from Hennessey went narrowly wide and Kevin Hector had a shot saved at the foot of a post. When Zeljeznicar tried to break away, John McGovern was alert to the danger and intercepted a potentially dangerous pass down the left.

The local press said the two-goal lead that Derby would take to Sarajevo was useful but not decisive. Gerald Mortimer wrote that Derby had risen to the occasion magnificently, as did the fans. 'There were not enough of them, but those who came made their presence felt,' he said. 'Those who stayed away were the unlucky ones.' Clough said he would have settled for a 1-0 lead after the first leg. Being two goals up was a tremendous bonus, he said. Derby's pace and precision had worried the opposition. 'It really grabbed you to watch such a display,' he added. The manager also emphasised the importance of the game. His pride at what had been achieved was clear to see. He reflected, 'The match occasion certainly helped us. There we were representing not just Derby but the whole country and playing among the cream.' Derby completed the job two weeks later, winning the away leg 2-1 with goals from John O'Hare and Alan Hinton.

22

European Cup: Second Round, First Leg
Derby County 3 Benfica 0
25 October 1972

What we saw last night was the cream on the cake.

Brian Clough always remembered this game for the complete satisfaction it gave him to beat one of the magical names of Continental football. He also smiled as he recalled watering the pitch the night before, to ensure the surface was nice and soft. It was in the days before sprinklers and Clough often told the story of how he used two big hosepipes to give the pitch a good soaking. On this occasion he fell asleep and by the time he woke up, the ground resembled a paddling pool. The president of FIFA, Sir Stanley Rous, told Clough he was surprised to see the pitch so muddy when there had hardly been any rain at his nearby hotel. The quick-thinking Derby boss explained it was a quirk of nature and that the Baseball Ground often had sudden downpours, while it stayed dry as a bone down the road. The sticky conditions and intense atmosphere proved too much for the Eagles of Lisbon, who returned home with their wings well and truly clipped. 'Don't ever try telling me there is nothing to be gained by falling asleep on the job,' Clough joked years later.

In preparation for the match, Clough travelled to Portugal to watch Benfica in action. He was not impressed. Even so, he did not tell the players. The last thing he wanted was for them to approach the game with any hint of complacency. Back in Derby, Clough took charge of a light training session on the day of the match, but gave away nothing to the press. 'There's nothing to say until ten past nine tonight,' he said. There was speculation that Derby would rest young defender Steve Powell who had played in the two previous League matches. Benfica manager Jimmy Hagan had watched Derby lose to Chelsea at Stamford Bridge in the League Cup earlier in the month. He said he was impressed by what he saw. 'They played some very good football,' he commented. 'They have so many good players, eleven good ones, in fact. The only fault was that they lost.' Hagan, who had started his career at Derby before joining Sheffield United, resisted naming his side in advance. He said he did not want his players to find out the line-up by reading a newspaper. Nevertheless, it was anticipated that the visitors would field the legendary Eusebio –

he had been the top goalscorer in the 1966 World Cup and was still expected to pose a massive threat to Derby's defence, having scored a hat-trick in a 5-0 win just a few days before this game. That result was one of seven successive victories, in which Benfica had scored a total of more than thirty goals and conceded just two. But in typical Clough style, Derby would not worry about the opposition; the visitors would have to worry about them instead. It was a philosophy that would serve the Master Manager very well throughout his career. 'Derby County will forget about Eusebio tonight,' said the *Derby Evening Telegraph*. 'They will concentrate purely and simply on attempting to beat Benfica by as many goals as possible in what promises to be a memorable European Cup match.' Anonymous letters writing off Derby's chances of victory were pinned-up on the Baseball Ground noticeboard by Peter Taylor. No further motivation was needed.

Derby County: Boulton, Robson, Daniel, Hennessey, McFarland, Todd, McGovern, Gemmill, O'Hare, Hector, Hinton.
Benfica: Jose Henriques, Malta Da Silva, Humberto, Messias, Adolfo, Jaime Graca, Nene, Toni, Baptista, Eusebio, Simoes. Sub used: Jordao.

Attendance: 38,100

Derby's performance in the first half was breathtaking. Add to that the electric atmosphere of a night match at a packed Baseball Ground, and you can understand why a newspaper report described it as one of the great European occasions. The tight construction of the stadium meant that the crowd was virtually within touching distance of the players. The terracing below the bright floodlights was steep, which allowed the noise of the fans to reverberate into a crescendo of excitement. If that was not intimidating enough for the visitors, then the attacking football that Derby played with classic precision that night certainly left Benfica reeling.

The Rams dominated so dramatically that they were 3-0 up by half-time. Roy McFarland headed the first goal from Alan Hinton's corner after just seven minutes, as Eusebio looked on in despair. The second goal also came from a corner. The ball glanced off McFarland's head and dropped to Kevin Hector whose first-time shot found its way into the top corner. John McGovern hit the third. Although Derby could not match their first half intensity after the break, with late Benfica pressure forcing Colin Boulton into making two great saves, the fans were more than happy to see the Rams take a 3-0 lead to Portugal. 'People came to see Eusebio,' wrote Gerald Mortimer in the *Derby Evening Telegraph*. 'They stayed to marvel at the power of Alan Hinton.' The newspaper's headline declared, 'Benfica Paralysed By Brilliant Rams'. Frank Clough of *The Sun* wrote, 'Dynamic Derby last night produced forty-five minutes of the finest quality attacking football I have ever seen from an English club in the European Cup.'

Derby fan Ron Stevenson remembers feeling proud to see the flag of European football flying at the Baseball Ground that night. 'I never thought I would see Derby in that position, representing the country in Europe. It was quite unbelievable,' said Ron, who founded the National and International branch of the Derby County Supporters Club. He said the atmosphere in the ground was unforgettable. 'The supporters did their best to help and encourage the players, it made them feel invulnerable. If you could have bottled that atmosphere, you would have had something very special. I think Benfica felt intimidated by it all. They lost it before they even had a chance. They were so shocked, they had never seen anything like it. I knew what a great player Eusebio was; I'd seen him play in the 1966 World Cup. Yet he hardly got a kick in the game.' Ron described the pitch as a sea of mud. 'I still can't understand how players like Kevin Hector could glide over the mud, but mortal players got stuck in it. We took Benfica apart and I came away from that match convinced we were going to do it, that we could actually win the European Cup.'

The day after the match, Clough told the press that his side had given Benfica 'something to think about'. Yet his priority quickly turned to the next match, at home to Sheffield United. 'The most important thing that happens in this club is a league match,' he said. 'What we saw last night was the cream on the cake.' He revealed that Hector had played with a bad back and had been on the treatment table until ten minutes before kick-off. Archie Gemmill was suffering a groin strain. Clough said that anyone looking for a reason why Derby had beaten Benfica should look at Hector and John O'Hare, who had run the visitors ragged.

For the second leg, Derby flew from East Midlands Airport with a verbal blast from Clough still ringing in their ears. The source of his irritation was Derby's poor away form and, in particular, a 4-0 defeat at Manchester City just days before their big game against Benfica. According to the press, no player was spared from criticism when Clough called them in to discuss the situation. Writing in the *Derby Evening Telegraph*, Gerald Mortimer described Derby's away record as a disgrace. In their previous four away matches in the League, the Rams had conceded fifteen goals and scored just one. The fans hoped that the trip to Portugal would be a completely different proposition. Gemmill, O'Hare and Hinton had all missed the match at Maine Road, but were restored to the side to face Derby's European opponents. Despite a three-goal lead, Clough was keen to ensure his players were not overconfident. 'Only an idiot could have felt complacent when he stepped out of the plane yesterday,' he said. After arriving at Lisbon Airport, the players were taken to Benfica's imposing Estadio da Luz to have a look round. 'It was important for the players to get the smell of the place,' said Clough. 'To get some impression of what they may face tomorrow night when it's full. I would take them three times a day if I could.' The manager, who disliked flying, also revealed he had made a special effort when choosing the team hotel. Their base was in a remote area that was little more than a village. 'I braved two flights to look at this hotel,' said Clough, 'and for me that is being very careful indeed.'

The preparation for the game was, again, typical Clough. Relaxation was the key. The players even enjoyed a paddle in the sea. Clough joined them and was so engrossed in conversation that a wave caught him by surprise and he was soaked from the waist down. Some members of the press joined the players for lunch and were apparently astonished by the relaxed atmosphere before such a crucial game. As far as the Benfica fans were concerned, their focus was on success in Europe and, with Eusebio recovered from an ankle injury, they remained optimistic. Clough delivered a classic one-liner when he summed-up his opponents' obsession with doing well in the European Cup: 'Certainly this competition is all that matters to Benfica because their domestic league is a joke.'

To emphasise the importance of relaxation, Clough lifted his no-smoking ban on the team coach and allowed Colin Boulton to have a cigarette on the way to the match. The low-key preparation paid off. Derby's defence withstood half an hour of intense Benfica pressure in a stadium full of more than 70,000 noisy fans and came away with a goalless draw. Derby fans who paid £34 for a two-day trip, including flights and a match ticket, were well rewarded. Even when the home side broke through the Rams' defence, Boulton was on top form and denied Eusebio a number of times. Afterwards, Clough acknowledged the battle his players had faced. 'Even if we'd been issued with those Belgian sub-machine guns, that they give to NATO, we couldn't have stopped them,' he said. 'There just seemed to be waves of red shirts.'

Derby's impressive rearguard action won praise in the British press. *The Sun* said that English football could be proud of its Champions, while the *Daily Mail* described the Rams as the most feared team left in the competition. In the *Daily Mirror* there was a special mention for the player who had been allowed a cigarette before kick-off. It reported,

> Derby were carried into the quarter finals on the shield provided by the bulk and bravery of their goalkeeper Colin Boulton. Boulton, the man who somehow seldom seems to receive his share of recognition, proved their most valuable player when Derby needed him most – in a first half of intense pressure...

Meanwhile, *The Guardian* reported that, by the hour-mark, the thousands of fans, like the Benfica players, sensed that there seemed no way through the visitors' defence. The newspaper's report said, 'It was indeed a superb performance from a team who had never experienced an atmosphere such as this and rarely the skilled ferocity of attacks from such a gifted side.' Clough said every player had given his all, but now their attention had to switch to the League. They would not be playing in Europe again for another five months.

23

FA Cup: Fourth Round Replay
Tottenham Hotspur 3 Derby County 5
7 February 1973

Even when we were 3-1 down near the end I hadn't written us off.

If ever there was a clear example of a Brian Clough side refusing to give up until the final whistle, this has to rank as probably the best. The fact it was against Tottenham Hotspur in the FA Cup makes it even more notable, given that it was Spurs who would eventually deny Clough the opportunity of winning the one trophy that eluded him throughout his illustrious career, nearly twenty years later. Many would say that it was actually poor refereeing in the 1991 final that denied Clough the chance of adding the FA Cup to his list of honours, but that is another story, told elsewhere in this catalogue of momentous matches.

Back in February 1973, Roger Davies had scored a late equaliser for Derby at the Baseball Ground to force a replay at White Hart Lane. On the same day as that 1-1 draw, the *Derby Evening Telegraph* published a collection of readers' letters replying to the newspaper's question asking whether Clough was the right man to take over as England manager. The national boss at the time, Sir Alf Ramsey, was not flavour of the month, despite winning the World Cup in 1966 and getting England to the quarter-finals of the competition in 1970. When it was announced that he was watching the FA Cup fourth-round tie in Derby, the news was roundly booed by fans in the ground. The letters in the local newspaper were emphatically in support of the idea of Clough becoming the national team manager, despite the fact it would have meant his departure from the Baseball Ground. Sixteen-year-old Kevin Hill from Derby said he wanted to see Clough become 'manager and Messiah of this dilapidated England outfit'. With words that would still resonate years later, the teenager added, 'England these days are living too much in the past ... Brian Clough has what this nation needs, which is the ability to assess quality.' Mrs K. Bryan from Kellington in Yorkshire wrote that Clough would bring 'a breath of fresh air' to the England team. She said he had the ability to keep the players on their toes and get the best out of them. There was no doubt he got the best out of the Derby players in this FA Cup replay against Spurs, although it did not appear so at first. The Rams won despite being 3-1 down with less than fifteen minutes to go.

Tottenham Hotspur: Jennings, Evans, Knowles, Pratt, England, Beal, Gilzean, Perryman, Chivers, Peters, Coates. Sub: Pearce.
Derby County: Boulton, Webster, Nish, Hennessey, McFarland, Todd, McGovern, Gemmill, Davies, Hector, O'Hare. Sub: Durban.

Attendance: 52,736

Goals from Martin Chivers and Alan Gilzean gave Spurs a 2-0 lead at half-time. Although Kevin Hector reduced the deficit, a disputed penalty scored by Mike England made it 3-1 to the home side. Some of their fans thought the game was over and left the stadium, while others stayed to chant 'Wembley, Wembley'. But Derby, playing in their yellow away shirts, were not finished. Young striker Roger Davies led what the *Derby Evening Telegraph* described as one of the greatest fightbacks in modern football. Two minutes after the penalty, Davies shot through a crowded goalmouth to score the first goal of what would be a memorable hat-trick, his first in senior football. His second goal was superbly taken. Controlling a cross from John O'Hare, he flicked the ball up and turned sharply to volley it into the roof of the net. BBC television commentator Barry Davies described it as a 'sweet turn and a fine goal'. It took the tie into extra time. Davies scored his hat-trick with a powerful header at the far post following a Hector corner on the right. That came two minutes into the second period of extra time. Derby were now in front for the first time in the game and their dominance left Spurs breathless. Six minutes later, a long clearance was headed on by Davies and Hector slid the ball past the advancing Pat Jennings to make it 5-3, at which point Barry Davies described it as 'surely one of the finest comebacks of all time in the FA Cup'.

After the match, the Derby players enjoyed what was described in the local newspaper as a quiet celebration drink, while Clough decided to go to bed early. Before he did, he briefly reflected on his side's never-say-die attitude. 'Even when we were 3-1 down near the end I hadn't written us off,' he said. 'How can you with the team playing the way they did? The lads were superb.' Spurs manager Bill Nicholson said his team was lucky that Derby had scored only five goals – it could have been more. 'It was a brilliant performance and although we were humiliated I am bound to say that justice was done,' said Nicholson. 'We simply collapsed and the floodgates opened.' Spurs midfielder Steve Perryman also praised the Rams. 'They murdered us in the second half and however painful it is to admit it, they gave a remarkable performance.'

Among the crowd that night was loyal Derby fan Ron Stevenson, who had gone to the game with a work colleague. 'He wanted to leave early, but I said we should stay,' said Ron. 'It was one of those nights when everything seemed to go against you and Derby could have capitulated so easily. But the players did not want to let Clough down and then face him at the end of the game. They just couldn't refuse him; he inspired them to achieve the impossible. It was absolutely amazing to watch – it's probably the best comeback I ever saw by Derby. I'm so glad I stayed until the final whistle to see it happen. It was one of those games that stays with you forever.'

The match was watched by the coach of Derby's fifth-round opponents, Queens Park Rangers. Bobby Campbell described a particular quality that would be a hallmark of Clough sides for years to come. 'It was the character in the Derby side that impressed me most,' remarked Campbell. 'They never lost their poise and they never stopped playing football.' The Rangers captain, Terry Venables, had also been watching. 'It's going to be very tough for us,' he said. 'Derby are fantastic.' Ironically, it was as manager of Spurs in 1991 that Venables clinched the FA Cup at Clough's expense. But Venables did not have the upper-hand in February 1973. Derby beat QPR 4-2 thanks to a hat-trick from Kevin Hector and another goal by Roger Davies. They were then beaten by Leeds United, who eventually lost in the final to Clough's former club, Sunderland.

Above: Clough and me.

Below: Derby County players with their thirty-two-year-old manager Brian Clough. Standing behind is his assistant Peter Taylor, October 1967. (© Trinity Mirror/ Mirrorpix/ Alamy Stock Photo)

FA Cup Quarter Final match at the Hawthorns. West Bromwich Albion 2 v Nottingham Forest 0. Forest manager Brian Clough watching the action from the bench, 11 March 1978. (© Trinity Mirror/ Mirrorpix/ Alamy Stock Photo)

European Cup Semi Final First Leg in Turin, Italy. Juventus 3 v Derby County 1. Derby manager Brian Clough, Peter Taylor and the rest of the Derby bench don't look overly happy with events unfolding on the pitch, 11 April 1973. (© Trinity Mirror/ Mirrorpix/ Alamy Stock Photo)

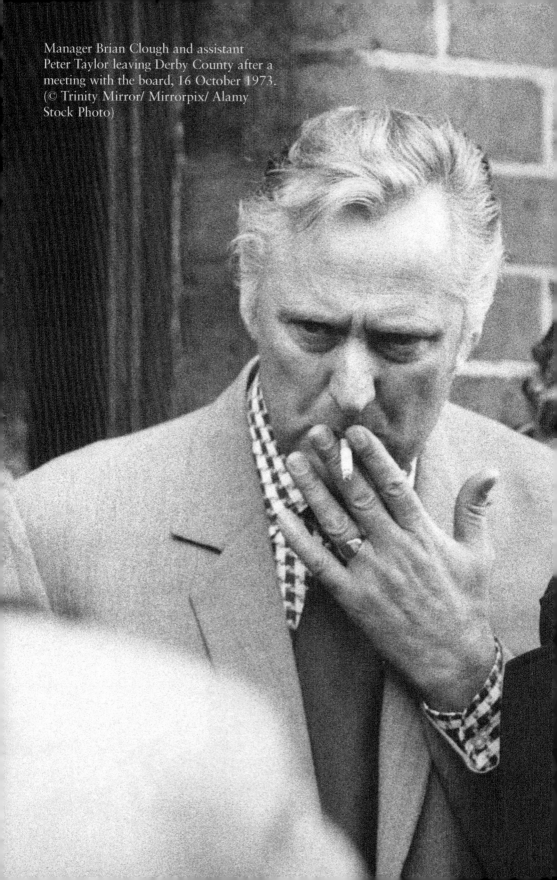

Manager Brian Clough and assistant Peter Taylor leaving Derby County after a meeting with the board, 16 October 1973. (© Trinity Mirror/ Mirrorpix/ Alamy Stock Photo)

Manager Brian Clough leaving Derby County after a meeting with the board,
16 October 1973. (© Trinity Mirror/ Mirrorpix/ Alamy Stock Photo)

24

European Cup Semi-final: First Leg
Juventus 3 Derby County 1
11 April 1973

I don't speak to cheating b*%***ds.

The controversial circumstances surrounding this defeat at the hands of the Italian champions would be a source of anger and frustration for Brian Clough for many years. Even in retirement he admitted that time had not eased the pain. He suspected it never would, even if he lived to be 100. Clough felt he had been cheated out of success in the European Cup. For a man who always ensured his teams played the game cleanly and without dissent towards referees, it was a match that left a nasty taste. His fury after the final whistle led to well-documented comments which were, to say the least, less than complimentary towards his Italian hosts. The remarks were unlikely to help his ambition of becoming England manager in the future.

Derby's preparation for the match included a few days of training – not in Italy but in the Spanish sunshine. As the game drew closer, Clough kept his cards very close to his chest. He decided not to name his line-up until shortly before kick-off. There was speculation over whether the Derby side would include Alan Hinton who had not played since the previous round of the competition against Spartak Trnava a month earlier, due to injury. But Clough decided not to risk him. It was also suggested that centre forward John O'Hare might be in the side due to Roger Davies' groin strain. After a training session in Turin, the Derby dressing room was said to be besieged by English and Italian journalists who were eager for information. Clough called in two representatives of the English press and told them to pass on what he had said to their colleagues. But on no account were they to convey any information to the Italians. 'They're telling us nothing,' he said, 'and we're letting nothing out to them.'

Clough had been to watch Juventus play Fiorentina but was disappointed by what he saw and concluded that the trip had been a waste of time. But he remained far more wary of Derby's Italian opponents than he was of Benfica in the second round. 'I went to Lisbon before we played Benfica and I saw enough then to realise that we could beat them and that Eusebio presented no sort of threat,' he said. 'This time, despite the dull nature of Italian league football, there is much more skill and tactical awareness to contend with.' Derby took Juventus legend John Charles with them as an advisor. He felt the home side had already passed their peak. 'At this stage of the season, Italian sides start to go physically,' said Charles. 'I think Derby can win this tie.'

The press speculated that Juventus would leave out their experienced international defender Luciano Spinosi. It was thought his place would be taken by Silvio Longobucco, who was considered to be more agile and quicker on the turn in order to cope with the threat of Kevin Hector. But the speculation proved to be unfounded. However, one name that was included among the home team was the future England manager Fabio Capello. Derby went into the game knowing that English clubs had gone to Italy in the European Cup on five previous occasions and had been beaten every time. Manchester United had lost twice to AC Milan, who also beat Ipswich. Everton and Liverpool had lost to Inter Milan. None of the English clubs had scored in those games. This match was a 72,000 sellout, with prices ranging from £1.25 for the cheapest standing tickets to £8 for seats.

Juventus: Zoff, Spinosi, Marchetti, Furino, Morini, Salvadore, Causio, Cuccureddu, Anastal, Capello, Altafini. Sub: Haller.
Derby: Boulton, Webster, Nish, Durban, McFarland, Todd, McGovern, Hector, O'Hare, Gemmill, Powell.

Attendance: 72,000

Juventus took the lead after twenty-eight minutes when their Brazilian veteran Jose Altafini controlled a high pass on the left and beat Ron Webster and Colin Todd before scoring with a clinical finish. Just two minutes later, Derby scored what they hoped would be a crucial away goal. Fed by O'Hare, Hector beat Salvadore and Morini and left Zoff sitting on the grass with a simple but expertly taken goal – the first by an English club in a European Cup match on Italian soil. In Tony Francis' book *There Was Some Football Too*, Hector recalled the goal:

> It came out of nothing at all. The ball was played up the left side and John O'Hare knocked it on to me. I took the ball into the box, shaped to shoot with my left foot but brought it inside and shot with my right. The ball flew into the net. It was a great feeling because British players just didn't get goals at Juventus. That was the equaliser and we held them well until half-time. After that, it got a bit too much for us.

The introduction of Juventus substitute Helmut Haller after sixty-two minutes lifted the home side. Causio scored and hit a post before Altafini got his second goal seven minutes from the end. Haller was at the centre of controversy after being spotted going into the referee's room before the match and at half-time. It incensed Clough and his assistant Peter Taylor, who suspected something fishy was going on. Their suspicions were raised when two Derby players, Roy McFarland and Archie Gemmill, were both booked for what appeared to be innocuous challenges. They were each already carrying yellow cards and would be out of the second leg. Jeff Farmer of the *Daily Mail* described the two cautions as 'scandalous'. In the *Daily Telegraph* Donald Saunders wrote, 'I doubt whether either player would have been shown the yellow card by the strictest referee in most matches.' While there was nothing to suggest the contact between Haller and the West German referee Gerhard Schulenberg had been improper, Clough felt cheated. After the game, he went to the mandatory press conference and waved the Italian press aside with the words, 'I don't speak to cheating b*%***ds!' The British journalist Brian Glanville of the *Sunday Times* had to translate the message in as tactful a way as he could. Clough's comments and lack of diplomacy on the international stage probably counted against him when he was interviewed for the England manager's job a few years later. Yet the frustration he felt inspired him to strive for success in the competition. 'We haven't finished yet by any means,' said Clough. 'Kevin's goal was vital to us.' Jose Altafini agreed with that assessment. While he accepted that a 3-1 victory was good for Juventus, he admitted he would have been happier with a 2-0 lead. If the scores were level at the end of the two legs, away goals would count double. The Italian journalists were confident their team had done enough to go through. The headline in the Milan newspaper *Corriere della Sera* declared, 'Altafini takes Juventus to the final'. According to another newspaper, *Il Giorno*, Clough had underestimated the Italians. A report in the *Derby Evening Telegraph* said Derby were now clinging to the European Cup by their fingernails.

European Cup Semi-final: Second Leg
Derby County 0 Juventus 0
25 April 1973

There's only one thing that's clear to me about tomorrow – this is going to be one hell of a tough match.

Facing a 3-1 deficit from the first leg, Brian Clough knew his Derby County side faced a mammoth task if they were to reach their first ever European Cup Final. Their vital away goal meant a 2-0 win at home would be enough. But Clough admitted Juventus were the best team Derby had faced in Europe. 'It is a situation which suits the Italians, but I honestly and sincerely believe that Derby County can reach the final,' he said. When it was suggested that Derby had done well to reach the semi-final, Clough responded in typical style: 'Well's not good enough. We must win tonight otherwise we could finish up having had a disgraceful season.'

The noisy arrival of hundreds of Juventus fans at East Midlands Airport signalled the prelude to this crucial match. Dressed in their black-and-white-striped shirts, a group of fans banged drums and cymbals while others carried banners and flags. On the morning of the game, the Juventus players went to the Baseball Ground to look at the pitch, which remained heavy due to rain. A UEFA official also inspected the pitch and said that with a dry day it would be perfect by the time the match kicked-off. Derby's team news was encouraging, especially considering the suspension of Roy McFarland and Archie Gemmill. Alan Hinton, Roger Davies and Ron Webster all declared themselves fit. Hinton, who had suffered a groin strain, had taken part in two reserve-team games in the previous ten days. Clough said Webster had made a remarkable recovery after missing the previous match against West Ham with a thigh strain. Davies had not featured in the first team since a 1-0 win over Arsenal before the first leg against Juventus. A groin muscle injury had now cleared up.

The *Derby Evening Telegraph*, in a special comment column, said the Derby supporters would play an important role in the outcome of the game. The fans could swing the result, it said, as the Rams strived for a glittering reward. 'Derby's task is colossal,' said another report previewing the game, 'but the players were in excellent heart before they trained this morning. They think that they can win and they are hoping for every last decibel of support from their supporters.' Clough said the Baseball Ground would be packed and he hoped the team would reward the crowd's faith. After the controversy surrounding the first leg, he added that he hoped the club would get 'a square deal' from the referee. The man in charge for this match was the Portuguese official, Francisco Lobo. An investigation by the *Sunday Times* later showed that Lobo had resisted a bribery attempt before the game. It appeared that a third party had tried, unsuccessfully, to tempt Lobo with five-thousand dollars and a Fiat car if the Italians won the second leg. The referee reported it to UEFA who subsequently exonerated Juventus of any wrongdoing.

On the same night as this memorable European match, television viewers had the chance to watch the flamboyant Larry Grayson, who had just been voted the funniest man on TV. Among his guests on the half-hour ITV show *Shut That Door* was Des O'Connor. Football fans were more interested to know whether the Italians would keep the door well and truly shut on Derby.

Derby County: Boulton, Webster, Nish, Powell, Daniel, Todd, McGovern, O'Hare, Davies, Hector, Hinton. Subs: Durban and Sims.
Juventus: Zoff, Spinosi, Marchetti, Furino, Morini, Salvadore, Causio, Cuccureddu, Anastasi, Capello, Altafini. Sub: Longobucco.

Attendance: 35,350

Derby put Juventus under the cosh straightaway as the game began at a storming pace. Within the first two minutes, Spinosi conceded a free-kick and Webster forced Dino Zoff to scramble to keep out a great shot. Zoff also blocked efforts from Hinton and O'Hare. Hinton threw his arms up in the air as if he had scored, as Zoff dived brilliantly to his left to turn a thunderous free-kick round the post. Such was Derby's domination that most of the game was played in or around the Juventus penalty area. Yet the home side were unable to score. Then came the moment when Derby had a superb opportunity to break the deadlock. It was the moment that could have turned the game. But it signalled a harsh reality that it just was not going to be Derby's night. The Rams were awarded a penalty after Spinosi tripped Kevin Hector. It was the Italians' twenty-fifth foul of the game. The usually dependable Hinton stepped up to take the spot-kick but struck the ball wide. Derby fan Ron Stevenson remembers watching the miss and feeling a sense of despair. 'It was virtually unknown for Hinton to miss a penalty,' he told me. 'It was the only decision that went our way – and we missed it. When I saw that happen, I knew it wasn't going to be our night.'

Six minutes after the penalty miss, Roger Davies was sent off for retaliation after clashing with centre half Morini. It meant Derby had to play the last twenty-seven minutes with ten men. 'That made a difficult task a virtual impossibility,' wrote Gerald Mortimer in his match report for the *Derby Evening Telegraph*. John Sims came on for Peter Daniel in the hopes of a last-gasp rally by Derby, but their European Cup dream was over. Clough said Davies would be fined a week's wages for his disgraceful behaviour. Nevertheless, a boxing promoter from Leicestershire was impressed with the striker and offered him the chance of becoming a professional boxer. The former RAF heavyweight champion Buddy Thomas was quoted as saying, 'I saw this lad on television last night and I liked his style.'

The national press gave Derby credit for the effort they showed in trying to break Juventus down. But the general feeling among the journalists was that the Rams had fallen well short of piercing a rigid defence. The *Daily Mirror* concluded, 'The bitter truth Derby had to face was that the Italian defensive system of man-for-man marking generally proved too tough for them to break down.' *The Guardian* suggested the Rams should have been more effective in front of goal: 'Had Derby's passing and shooting been remotely comparable with their endeavour the story might have been so different.'

After missing the penalty, Hinton received no words of comfort from Clough, who criticised him for ignoring orders and not playing wide enough to stretch the Juventus defence. Hinton replied by telling the local press that he did not want to get into a public slanging match and that he still regarded Clough as the best manager in the business. Hinton added, 'I'm not going to let what happened in one match destroy something that's been built up over the years.' Clough left the ground that night with feelings of disappointment and frustration, combined with the anger he still felt from the first leg. Although he would not secure the ultimate prize during his time at Derby, within just six years he would make the dream a reality at local rivals Nottingham Forest.

26

Division One
Manchester United 0 Derby County 1
13 October 1973

In the end, my pride and conceit took over.

The events that followed this victory at Old Trafford triggered one of the most dramatic moments in Brian Clough's career. He and his assistant Peter Taylor resigned from Derby County over a boardroom bust-up. It could be considered that what happened on the pitch paled into insignificance compared with the shocking developments afterwards. But it was the satisfaction of securing their first away win of the season that tempted Clough and Taylor to take the unusual decision to venture into the United boardroom after the game. Clough said later he had gone there against his better judgement. It seems that what happened in that room played a key part in the pair's decision to tender their resignations two days later. It turned out to be the biggest regret of Clough's career.

According to the press, in their preview of the game it was a crucial fixture for Derby. The *Derby Evening Telegraph* said that after defeats at Liverpool, Coventry City and Tottenham Hotspur since the start of the season, Derby had to start picking up points away from home if they were to keep in touch with the top of the table. A 1-1 draw with Norwich early in October had left Derby in fourth position. That was followed by a 2-2 draw at home to Clough's former club, Sunderland, in the League Cup. In the same competition, Manchester United were knocked-out by Middlesbrough, losing 1-0 at Old Trafford. United named Scottish international defender Alex Forsyth in their team against Derby, for his first League match of the season. For Derby, Roy McFarland had received treatment for a slight knee strain and was named in the same line-up that had drawn with Sunderland.

Manchester United: Stepney, M. Buchan, Forsyth, Greenhoff, Holton, James, Morgan, Young, Kidd, Anderson, Graham. Sub: G. Buchan.
Derby County: Boulton, Webster, Nish, Newton, McFarland, Todd, McGovern, Gemmill, Davies, Hector, Hinton. Sub: O'Hare.

Attendance: 43,724

A Kevin Hector goal after just four minutes was enough to give Derby the win they needed. Forsyth had tried to pass the ball back to Stepney but Hector spotted an opportunity and placed his shot in the far corner. It took United forty minutes to produce an effort on goal that called Boulton into action, catching Graham's header under the bar. The home side stepped up their threat in the second half. With twelve minutes to go, a shot by Kidd hit the bar as Boulton watched helplessly. Young latched onto the rebound but the ball hit the bar once again and Derby knew that luck was on their side. However, off the pitch fortune was not smiling on them. Just as Clough was building an empire that could have dominated football in the 1970s and beyond, it all came crashing down.

In his first autobiography, Clough recalled how he and Taylor decided to go into the United boardroom after the game, because winning at Old Trafford did not happen very often. Clough was reluctant to go there as he was not the type to hobnob with directors, but he agreed to Taylor's suggestion. As the champagne was poured, Taylor took exception to one of the Derby directors, Jack Kirkland, pointing his finger towards him and asking for a meeting. Kirkland wanted to know exactly what Taylor's role was at the club. Later Clough wrote, 'When Kirkland crooked his beckoning finger at Taylor he was effectively squeezing the trigger.' For Clough and Taylor this was a step too far and the manager tendered their resignations.

Clough's relationship with Derby chairman Sam Longson had been strained for some time. Initially, Longson had treated Clough like the son he never had. But things turned sour between them as Derby became more successful and Clough appeared increasingly on the television and in the newspapers, with his usual outspoken comments making the headlines. Although the public was keen to hear what the entertaining manager had to say, Longson wanted Clough to curtail his media work because he felt it was to the detriment of the club. Yet Derby had continued to be successful even with Clough maintaining his media commitments. The manager was not going to change.

As reporters gathered at the Baseball Ground, eager for further quotes on a story that now made front-page news, a television journalist asked Clough why he had resigned. 'There's not enough time, there's not enough film, there's a million reasons,' he replied. He was then asked, 'Where do you go from here?' The answer was simple. 'I'm going for my lunch – you get off home for yours.' In 2004, Clough was asked in *Four Four Two* magazine to explain the real reason for his fallout with Longson. He said Derby's success had gone to the chairman's head. Clough added,

He was upset that I couldn't be bothered going to board meetings and started to believe he ran Derby County. In the end, my pride and conceit took over.

Towards the end, I threw a bunch of keys at him because he'd locked the bar at the Baseball Ground and I wanted to give someone a drink. But there was no set reason for the break, we just disagreed too often near the end.

Although the victory at Old Trafford was to be Clough's last match as Derby manager, his comments to the press after the game gave no hint of the drama that was about to unfold. That evening he was still talking about Derby's forthcoming matches. He even thought about Don Revie studying the top of the League to see who posed the major threat to Leeds. Clough told the press, 'He'll be thinking about Liverpool or Newcastle. But one club will hit him in the eye. Us. And I reckon we'll be ready when they come to Derby at the end of November.' By then, however, Dave Mackay was in charge at the Baseball Ground. Despite fans protesting about Clough and Taylor's departure and the players writing to the board to demand the reinstatement of the pair, Mackay's move from local rivals Nottingham Forest was confirmed before the end of October. Jimmy Gordon was placed in temporary charge for the next game against Leicester City, at which Clough made a surprise appearance. Arriving in a Rolls-Royce, he entered the Baseball Ground through the players' entrance and made his way to the B Stand. Looking slightly pensive initially, he raised an arm and waved to the fans who cheered him. At one point, Longson also stood up and waved, assuming that the cheers were for him. After a few minutes, Clough left the ground and made his way to London in order to appear on the Michael Parkinson television chat show that evening.

A headline in the *Derby Evening Telegraph* described it as 'The Worst Week In The Rams' History'. Gerald Mortimer wrote that the storm clouds had been gathering for some time. The crunch, he said, had come on the Monday afternoon after the match against United, when Clough and Taylor had received a letter from Longson. The board said it did not want to stop Clough appearing on television or writing for newspapers, but wanted to be told each time he intended to do so. 'They were not stopping him, rather, it would seem, imposing a slow process of strangulation,' wrote Mortimer. Letters to the newspaper were said to be overwhelmingly in favour of the management duo. T. M. Green asked, 'Why is it that a manager who is 100 per cent a crowd favourite, and 100 per cent respected and supported by the players, be forced to resign?' Clough told the story of his resignation to the *Daily Mail* and posed for a photograph with the newspaper's sports writer, Jeff Farmer. Pointing to a potted plant at the Baseball Ground, Clough said, 'We planted a seed, it's a healthy plant now. I wish we could have stayed around to see the fruit.'

27

Division Three
Brighton 2 Bristol Rovers 8
1 December 1973

It was the most humiliating ninety minutes of my career.

The scoreline of this match was to be etched on Brian Clough's memory as deeply as the two European Cup finals he was to win a few years later. It was certainly a shock to the system for him, after enjoying tremendous success with Derby only a few months before. The opportunity to lead Brighton had given him a swift return to management following his dramatic departure from the Baseball Ground. Even though he stayed at Brighton for only eight months, Clough denied it was a stopgap appointment between jobs. In his autobiography *Walking on Water*, he stressed that he was sincere in his agreement with the Brighton chairman, Mike Bamber, who he described as the finest chairman he had worked for. In an interview with his friend Brian Moore for the video *Cloughie – The Brian Clough Story*, Clough admitted he had gone to Brighton for the money. When he and his assistant Peter Taylor were appointed in October 1973, Brighton were twentieth in Division Three. There was clearly a lot of work to do in order to lift the ailing club towards any possibility of promotion. Within the first few weeks, the size of the task was all too obvious when Brighton lost 4-0 to non-League side Walton and Hersham in the first round of the FA Cup. Clough later described it as one of his worst days in football. The situation did not get much better when, a few days later, Brighton lost 8-2 at home to high-flying Bristol Rovers in the League. Commentating on the match, Brian Moore described it as 'a most remarkable game of football'. A frustrated Clough, who was joined in the dugout by his young sons Simon and Nigel for some of the game, did not hold back in the press conference afterwards.

Brighton: Powney, Templeman, Ley, Spearitt, Gall, R. Howell, Towner, Beamish, Hilton, Robertson, O'Sullivan. Sub: G. Howell
Bristol Rovers: Eadie, Jacobs, Parsons, Green, Taylor, Prince, Fearnley, Stanton, Warboys, Bannister, Dobson. Sub: John.

Attendance: 10,762

For those TV viewers who loved seeing goals, and plenty of them, this game was a real dream. But for Brighton's fans it turned into a nightmare, as they watched two opposition players score hat-tricks. They were Alan Warboys and Bruce Bannister, who gained a cult following among Rovers fans with the nicknames 'Smash and Grab'. Warboys was a target man, an old-fashioned, imposing centre forward who became known as 'Smash'. The smaller Bannister was ready to capitalise on any chances and earned the nickname 'Grab'. Remembering the match years later, Bannister recalled that the ground was packed because all the games in the London area that day had been called off due to bad weather. He told *Observer Sport Monthly* that once Chelsea's match against unbeaten Leeds was postponed, all the attention turned to this game. The dynamic duo combined brilliantly for the first goal after four minutes. Warboys ran down the left wing, beat Gall near the byline and Bannister timed his run well to open the scoring. After another Rovers goal, Brighton pulled it back to 2-1 with a fine right-foot shot from O'Sullivan. The visitors then ramped up the pressure and were 5-1 up by half-time thanks to two more goals from Bannister and one from Warboys, who headed home a cross from the left by Dobson.

The second half picked up from where the first had finished, with Warboys dominating the play up front for Rovers. He completed his hat-trick on sixty-three minutes before scoring a fourth seven minutes later. Ronnie Howell scored for Albion on eighty-seven minutes, but the humiliation in front of the television cameras was already complete. Ironically, all the goals had been scored by players in Albion shirts because Rovers were wearing Brighton's second strip. The television producers had decided that Rovers' usual red-and-white away kit would look too similar to Brighton's blue-and-white stripes for viewers watching in black and white.

The final score could easily have been 9-2 if a fierce left-foot shot by Warboys had gone in rather than hitting the bar. In 2006, Warboys described it as an unbelievable performance. He told *Observer Sport Monthly*, 'I finished with a cut eye and needed stitches. While I was on the treatment table Cloughie walked in. He told me that the cut must have been self-inflicted, because his defenders hadn't been near me all afternoon.'

Commenting after the match, Clough described it as the most humiliating ninety minutes of his career. 'I was ashamed for the town and the club that eleven players could play like that,' he said. 'I feel sick. We were pathetic. This side hasn't got enough heart to fill a thimble. There are no magic wands.'

The following day, Clough appeared on ITV's *The Big Match* to analyse the defeat. It is hard to imagine a Premier League manager being prepared to sit in a television studio these days to talk openly and in detail about such a hefty loss. In fact, Brian Moore suggested to his guest that there had been speculation in the office about whether or not he would turn up for the programme, such was the embarrassment about the result. 'Obviously they were wrong and they don't know me,' replied Clough with a smile. He admitted it had been a shattering defeat, especially as his young family was in town house-hunting, but he was prepared to face the music. He told Moore, 'You get up the next morning, the sun was shining and here I am wanting to talk football and wanting to discuss Brighton and any other aspect of the game you would like.' Looking at footage of some of the goals his side had conceded, he said the first goal had been 'a killer' because it was scored so early in the game. Poor marking was to blame, he said, and he felt sorry for his goalkeeper who 'didn't stand a prayer'. He said his players had 'caved in' under the pressure. 'We were not keen on defending,' he said. 'It takes heart to defend, as well as skill and ability.' In his autobiography *Walking on Water*, Clough said the Brighton players had been frightened of him. In fact, he described them as being petrified. If anything, this match served to disprove the theory that his successful, trophy-winning teams were motivated by fear. Surely if they had been, they too would have 'caved in' as the Brighton players did that day. Clough insisted that his teams at Derby County and Nottingham Forest could not have produced the type of football they displayed if they had been frightened. He said, 'There was not an ounce of fear in their game – they played with a kind of freedom and sheer joy that you rarely see from teams today.' Brighton fans, on the other hand, may well have feared for the future after the trouncing by Bristol Rovers.

In the *Brighton Argus*, the Albion reporter John Vinnicombe said it was a day that would be recalled by the club's fans with 'infinite pain'. Describing Albion as the sick men of Division Three, Vinnicombe warned that the club was in need of such dramatic surgery, it could cause lasting damage in the process. 'The danger at the Goldstone is that the cure prescribed by Dr Clough might kill the patient,' he wrote. He then assessed the size of the challenge confronting Clough: 'To rebuild is his task, and in view of the massive structural weaknesses, he has to demolish the very foundations of the side and begin afresh. In the process Albion will lose more matches, but never, let it be hoped, surrender as they did against Rovers.'

Brighton's captain under Clough, Norman Gall, said he enjoyed playing for the new manager. Gall is quoted in *The Life of Brian* by Tim Crane and said, 'He knew exactly what he wanted, who was good, who was bad and what they could and couldn't do.' Gall said that after the 8-2 defeat he had expected to receive a rollicking. 'Instead, he told me not to worry about it, go home and have a drink and that I was playing next week.'

Clough insisted that he and Taylor would not be rushed into making new signings. 'If we've got to sit through 8-2 defeats for the next six weeks before the type of player we require comes on the market, we'll do just that,' he said. The closing pictures of *The Big Match* showed Clough sitting alone in the dugout. Brian Moore, with young Nigel on his knee in the studio, introduced a recap of the Rovers goals, which he said had left 'our old friend Brian, such a lonely man down in Brighton yesterday'. Brighton slipped to one place above the relegation zone after further defeats to Tranmere, Watford and Aldershot.

New signings were made and after a number of victories in the New Year they climbed up the table. Optimism in some quarters prompted Clough to comment, 'So, people are talking about the mathematical possibility of us going up. Well listen to me. We couldn't go up if we had Einstein on our side – and he was pretty good at figures.' Clough's final match in charge of Brighton was at Bristol Rovers and he vowed that they would not lose 8-2 again. He was right, with the match ending in a 1-1 draw after a late Rovers equaliser. Despite his short stay on the south coast, Clough proved to be the catalyst for Brighton's transformation. Peter Taylor remained at the Goldstone Ground after Clough left in July 1974 and took them to fourth in the table. Brighton went on to win promotion to Division Two in 1977 under Alan Mullery.

28

FA Charity Shield
Leeds United 1 Liverpool 1
(Liverpool won 6-5 on penalties)
10 August 1974

They were ready to eat me alive.

When Kevin Keegan and Billy Bremner took off their shirts and threw them to the ground in disgust after being sent off in this Wembley showpiece, it marked a new low-point for English football. The game also marked the start of what was to be the lowest point in Brian Clough's managerial career. His forty-four days at Leeds United have been well documented over the years, but this match clearly demonstrated his detachment from the Leeds side he had previously criticised so openly. The game displayed the type of football Clough despised. It was cynical, ugly and generally ill-tempered, with little entertainment on show. And that was from both teams.

Clough had often spoken about his dislike of Leeds' disciplinary record under manager Don Revie and had called for the club to be relegated as punishment. Yet when Revie left Elland Road to become England manager, United's board of directors wanted a big name to replace him – so they chose Clough. He accepted the job knowing it gave him the opportunity of once again competing for the European Cup, having felt he was cheated out of the competition at Derby. Clough later joked that he did not stay long enough at Leeds to have his own teacup, never mind the European Cup. He admitted that he had underestimated the level of resentment waiting for him at Leeds, despite recognising the talent of players like Billy Bremner and Johnny Giles, and that he had tried to change things too quickly. It has been well documented, again, that he told the Leeds players they could throw their medals in the bin because they had not won them fairly.

In his autobiography, *Walking on Water*, Clough stated he did not feel the remotest connection with the Leeds players. So he telephoned Revie before the Charity Shield match against Liverpool to offer him the opportunity of leading out his League Champions at Wembley. When Revie declined, it meant that it was a reluctant Clough who walked out alongside Bill Shankly in front of the two teams. As they entered the stadium, the new Leeds boss applauded the tough-talking Scotsman who had rebuilt the Merseyside club so successfully and was now taking his ceremonial bow as manager. Years later, Clough said that walking alongside Shankly while leading out the Leeds team was one of the most treasured moments of his career. He felt privileged to be close to one of the greatest football men he had ever met. But Clough admitted there was no sense of togetherness among the Leeds players who walked out behind him. They had the glummest faces ever seen at such an occasion, he said.

Leeds United: Harvey, Reaney, McQueen, Hunter, Cherry, Lorrimer, Bremner, Giles, E. Gray, Clarke, Jordan. Sub: McKenzie.
Liverpool: Clemence, Smith, Thompson, Hughes, Lindsay, Heighway, Cormack, Hall, Callaghan, Keegan, Boersma.

Attendance: 67,000

It was the first time the Charity Shield, between the League Champions and the FA Cup holders, had been televised and held at Wembley. The intention was to present the perfect image of English football to a worldwide audience. But there were times when the match descended into a circus, with the players showing the very worst the game could offer. Within minutes of the kick-off there were niggling fouls and frayed tempers. 'It was if the players were offering grounds for all my criticism that they had resented so much,' reflected Clough. The bad feeling between both sets of players culminated in Keegan and Bremner being sent off after a brawl early in the second half. Both players took off their shirts and flung them to the ground as they left the pitch. The BBC television commentator Barry Davies questioned the players' behaviour. Watching the first British footballers to be sent off at Wembley, he said that dismissing the referee's authority in that manner could not be good for the game. 'This is a face of English football we did not want to see,' remarked Davies. Clough said he had been disgusted by the incident and what he called 'the dirty tactics' of his players who, he said, had aimed to provoke Keegan. The new Leeds boss told a journalist how he felt and the comments were published. 'After that, I was on the way out at Elland Road,' reflected Clough in 2001. There were also bookings for Liverpool's Tommy Smith and United's Giles before the game ended in a 1-1 stalemate. Leeds had gone 1-0 down after a goal from Phil Boersma in the first half, but equalised through a Trevor Cherry header which beat the diving Clemence on seventy minutes.

Liverpool won the subsequent penalty shoot-out 6-5 when Leeds goalkeeper David Harvey missed his spot-kick and Liverpool's Ian Callaghan hit the ball home emphatically. As the players gathered together Clough, who had been sitting alongside Shankly during the game, put a consoling hand on Harvey's back. Just over a month later, the hand of fate was on Clough's back when he was sacked and handed a substantial cheque by Leeds. The club's chairman Manny Cussins told the waiting media, 'What has been done is for the good of the club. The club and the happiness of the players must come first. Nothing can be successful unless the staff is happy.' On further questioning he said they had been spoilt by Don Revie. As Clough left Elland Road, he said it was a bad day for Leeds and a bad day for football. But it was not bad for his bank balance. Leeds paid-up his contract in full and also agreed to pay the tax, as well as allowing him to keep the new Mercedes they had given him. For the first time in his life Clough was financially secure and would be able to tackle his next challenge without fear of the sack. He would be able to do things his way. Although Leeds reached the European Cup Final in 1975 under the management of Jimmy Armfield, they were unable to win the coveted trophy. In the following years, Clough did win the European Cup - not once, but twice. When he died in 2004, among the items left in tribute at Nottingham Forest's City Ground was a Leeds shirt with a message written on it: 'Our loss for the second time.'

29

Anglo-Scottish Cup: Final, Second Leg
Nottingham Forest 4 Leyton Orient 0
15 December 1976

Those people who think it will be easy don't know what they are talking about. This tie is far from over…

The significance of this victory in a minor cup competition can never be underestimated in Cloughie's exciting journey to European glory at Nottingham Forest. He was only too well aware it would give his new team their first taste of winning a trophy. It may not have been the most celebrated of tournaments, but the experience of winning silverware cemented a belief within the players that they were capable and worthy of success – and that the master manager was the one who could lead them to even greater riches.

The Anglo-Scottish Cup had been introduced the previous season. Sixteen English clubs were put into four groups, with the winner of each group qualifying for the knockout stages against four Scottish teams who had won two-legged qualifying rounds. Clough's hometown team Middlesbrough were the cup holders, but finished runners-up in their group this time, behind Newcastle United. Forest won their group and were one of only two sides to collect extra points for the number of goals they scored. Teams who scored three goals in a game were awarded an extra point. The Reds did that twice, beating West Bromwich Albion 3-2 and Bristol City 4-2.

After victory over Kilmarnock in the quarter-final and Ayr United in the semi-final, Forest faced Leyton Orient in the two-legged final. The first leg was away at Brisbane Road on 13 December 1976 and continued the Reds' unbeaten record in the capital since Clough had taken over in January 1975. They had already beaten Orient by a single goal in a League match earlier in the season and they went into the first leg undefeated in twelve games in London since Clough's arrival. His first match in charge had been a victory over Spurs at White Hart Lane in a third-round FA Cup replay.

Clough had a fifteen-man squad to choose from for the match at Orient, including seventeen-year-old goalkeeper Chris Woods, who would make a name for himself in a Wembley final less than two years later. He was a substitute for the first leg, behind first choice John Middleton. Forest took the lead with a John Robertson penalty in the twenty-eighth minute. Colin Barrett, who came on as a substitute for the injured Peter Withe, chipped the ball forward and Orient's Phil Hoadley handled in the penalty area. The World Cup referee, Jack Taylor, awarded the spot-kick and Robertson beat John Jackson with a low shot to the 'keeper's right. Despite Forest's general dominance during the game, coming close to a second goal with several headers by Larry Lloyd and a shot from John McGovern which whistled over the bar, they conceded a last-minute equaliser when Derek Possee headed home from a cross. At 5 feet 6 inches tall, Possee was the smallest player on the field, but he could still outjump most centre halves. His goal gave George Petchey's side a glimmer of hope as both sides met again just two days later for the crucial second leg at the City Ground.

Nottingham Forest: Middleton, Anderson, Clark, McGovern, Lloyd, Chapman, O'Neill, Barrett, Bowery, Bowyer, Robertson (Gunn). Sub: Woods.
Leyton Orient: Jackson, Payne, Roffey, Bennett, Hoadley, Roeder, Whittle, Grealish, Possee, Queen, Allder (Fisher). Sub: Smeulders.
Referee: R. Mathewson

Attendance: 12,717

Forest went into the match with several of their key players injured. Peter Withe, Tony Woodcock and John O'Hare were unable to be included. It meant Clough was unable to confirm his side until just before kick-off. Orient also had injury worries because winger Laurie Cunningham, who went on to play for West Bromwich Albion and England, pulled a muscle in the first game.

While the Reds were favourites to lift their first trophy in many years, Clough warned against overconfidence among players and fans. He admitted his side had played remarkably well in the first leg and had been unlucky not to bring a lead back to the City Ground, but he stressed the tie would not be easy and that the visitors would put up a fight. Yet his eagerness to win the cup was undeniable and he said it was important for the players too, not least because they would receive a substantial bonus!

Forest certainly turned on the style at the City Ground. Colin Barrett was in the starting line-up this time and scored two of the Reds' four goals in the kind of display that would whet the appetite for promotion to Division One.

The reserve striker Bert Bowery was brought in and caused a headache for the Orient defence. Right-back Viv Anderson teamed-up well with Martin O'Neill in a partnership that would continue to serve Forest brilliantly in the coming years. The visitors, who were bottom of Division Two, were simply outclassed.

The first goal came in the fifteenth minute from Barrett who ran through from midfield, received the ball from Ian Bowyer and struck it past Jackson. The lead was doubled shortly after half an hour when former captain Sammy Chapman, playing in midfield, headed an O'Neill free-kick towards the goal. Jackson failed to hold the ball and Chapman hammered in the rebound. Forest were 3-0 up by half-time after more impressive work from Barrett. He was brought down outside the Orient area by Peter Bennett. McGovern tapped the resulting free-kick to Barrett who unleashed an unstoppable shot into the top corner of the net.

Bryn Gunn was brought on as an emergency outside left to replace the injured John Robertson at half-time, but most of Forest's attacks went down the right. The Reds' fourth goal came in the sixty-third minute when Bowyer, playing in a striking role, latched on to a through ball from O'Neill to score against his former club. Barrett nearly grabbed a hat-trick but his volley from an O'Neill corner was kept out by Jackson. Despite that miss, Forest won the game and the cup comfortably. The aggregate score was 5-1. John Lawson wrote in the *Nottingham Evening Post* that Forest were playing so fluently that they could even carry him in the side. He also suggested, quite accurately, that promotion was probably just around the corner. Forest returned to Division One in 1977 and in the club's newly reintroduced Year Book the chairman Brian Appleby was full of praise for the manager. He wrote,

> Ever since Brian Clough came to the City Ground there has been an ever-increasing atmosphere of optimism – he is one of those rare people who has about him a charisma which inspires confidence, motivates everybody who works with him and, above all else, possesses ability to combine it with boundless enthusiasm.

Clough later revealed that winning the Anglo-Scottish Cup had meant a lot to him, as it meant getting his hands on a trophy. He admitted that his team probably travelled for more minutes than there were people in the grounds for the visits to Ayr and Kilmarnock, but at least there was something tangible to enjoy at the end – even though injuries picked up along the way could have hindered the club's promotion prospects. Referring to the Anglo-Scottish Cup, Clough told a *Nottingham Evening Post* supplement, published to celebrate promotion to Division One, 'I know it wasn't exactly a crowning glory but a lot of effort went into getting that trophy and we had something to mark the achievement.'

30

Division One
Manchester United 0 Nottingham Forest 4
17 December 1977

That was the absolute pinnacle, if we had realised it at the time...

Clough is often described as 'the best manager England never had'. It was in December 1977 that he went along to the Football Association's headquarters at Lancaster Gate and was interviewed for the job of England boss. After the seventy-five-minute interview, Forest fans were left with an anxious wait to see whether they would lose their manager. Clough was certainly a popular choice among supporters around the country, but the Football Association had other ideas and appointed Ron Greenwood, announcing their decision around a week after the interviews. It was a decision that would continue to rankle the outspoken Clough in the years to come. Yet on the pitch Forest were going from strength to strength and hit top gear just a few days after the England announcement. The First Division leaders trounced the FA Cup holders Manchester United at Old Trafford. The performance and result were important because they gave the players and the fans the belief they could actually win the title. In his book *The Life of Brian*, Tim Crane describes the game as one of the greatest Forest performances of all time. He comments, 'It was as though ten years of management had come to fruition on a winter's afternoon...' The significance of the result was emphasised when United went on to beat second-placed Everton on Boxing Day.

David Needham made his debut in the Forest defence. The centre half was signed from Queens Park Rangers for £150,000 as a replacement for Larry Lloyd who had broken a bone in his foot in the previous league match against Coventry. Needham was well known in the Nottingham area, having spent eleven years at neighbours Notts County, before joining QPR.

Nottingham Forest: Shilton, Anderson, Barrett, McGovern, Needham, Burns, O'Neill, Gemmill, Withe, Woodcock, Robertson. Sub: Bowyer.

Manchester United: Roche, Nicholl, Houston, McIlroy, B. Greenhoff, Buchan, Coppell, J. Greenhoff, Pearson, Macari, Hill. Sub: Grimes.

Attendance: 54,374

Forest withstood a great deal of early pressure from the home side, who almost went ahead within two minutes through an effort from Sammy McIlroy that went wide. Following a further United attack, Needham had to head the ball out for a corner. Peter Shilton was also called into action and punched the ball clear after a cross from Gordon Hill. The pressure on the Forest defence was eased when a shot from Peter Withe was deflected for a corner. A Kenny Burns header was then saved by Paddy Roche. For a brief spell it looked like Needham's debut might be one to forget. He was booked in the seventeenth minute for bringing down Jimmy Greenhoff from behind. Fortunately, it was not long before Forest began to stamp their authority on the game and silenced the home fans. They took the lead in the twenty-third minute when a Tony Woodcock shot from a tight angle hit the post and rebounded into the net off Brian Greenhoff.

Shortly after Forest's opening goal, the home side brought on Ashley Grimes to replace the injured striker Stuart Pearson. But United's problems increased when Forest went 2-0 up within half an hour. A cross from John Robertson was flicked to Woodcock, who hammered the ball high into the net in front of the Stretford End. Forest, playing in their yellow away strip, were exposing weaknesses in the United defence with wave after wave of attacks. Viv Anderson had a shot at goal but was off-target and Woodcock forced Roche to make a reflex save. Although Forest were two goals in front at half-time, United were fortunate not to be further behind.

In the second half, Forest continued to dictate the pace of the game and looked like scoring with every attack. The third goal owed a great deal to the tremendous work of Archie Gemmill. United had a free-kick near the edge of the Forest penalty area. The shot was blocked and Gemmill's tireless running meant he broke away from the halfway line, nutmegged the approaching Jimmy Nicholl and delivered a perfectly weighted pass to Robertson. The winger rounded Roche and slipped the ball into an empty net in the fifty-third minute. As the quick, slick and entertaining Forest continued to press United with some delightful one-touch football, McGovern had a shot deflected for a corner and the unmarked Anderson had only the 'keeper to beat but blasted the ball over the bar. Forest's fourth goal came from more enterprising work by Gemmill, whose defence-splitting pass sent Woodcock one-on-one with Roche. The striker kept his cool and slipped the ball home in the eighty-ninth minute.

The BBC *Match of the Day* commentator Barry Davies described United as being 'buried in their own backyard'. In the book *Forest Giants* by John McGovern and Rob Jovanovic, Clough reflected on the victory by saying, 'That was the absolute pinnacle, if we had realised it at the time, but we took it step by step. There was a spell between us getting the third and the fourth and I said, "I'm glad that's gone in just to let people know we could have had ten" – and we could have had ten! That's how much Manchester United were inferior to us.'

The *Daily Mail's* Ronald Crowther was full of praise for the Reds' performance. He wrote, 'After an early attacking flurry by United had proved unproductive, Forest took them apart in the tactical sense and exploited flaws that are in need of urgent attention.' He named Peter Shilton as the key man in that operation and described how the England goalkeeper spotted United's full-backs wide out on the wings and cut out their midfield by placing his clearances near the edge of the opposition penalty area. At that point, Withe and Woodcock beat the Manchester defenders in the air. Crowther said the two strikers had struck terror in the heart of the defence with brilliant support from McGovern and Gemmill. Crowther added, 'It was a team performance by Clough's men to silence the cynics who claim that Forest are in a false position. And for any of their rivals who might nurture any such notions I've got three words of advice – stop fooling yourselves.'

After the match, David Needham admitted he had been a little apprehensive about the game but now realised he should not have been. In the 1979 *Nottingham Forest Annual*, Needham said everything had worked perfectly in the game against United. 'For actual football skill that is the best team performance I have experienced in all my years as a professional,' he said. Quoted in the same publication, Viv Anderson, who had been a Manchester United fan as a boy, described it as an outstanding memory. Anderson said, 'As we walked off at the end Tony Woodcock, John Robertson and myself looked at each other. For all we could hear was the Forest crowd's cheers. We had actually silenced the Stretford End, and that takes some doing.'

Clough told the *Nottingham Evening Post* after the game that his side could have had 'a hatful'. Describing it as 'a massacre', he said the result could easily have been of 'incredible proportions'. While impressed with Needham's debut, he joked, 'I think he is a very lucky young man to be coming into a side like this.'

31

League Cup Final
Liverpool 0 Nottingham Forest 0
18 March 1978

They are my Wembley virgins.

As Brian Clough led out his Nottingham Forest team at Wembley, he broke with convention and signalled to his players to stop for a moment to acknowledge the fans who had turned out in their thousands to cheer them on. The Liverpool boss Bob Paisley continued walking a couple of steps before he realised that Clough had stopped. He waited patiently for the Forest manager to catch up with him. It was a piece of Clough magic which let the players savour the special atmosphere in the historic stadium and, at the same time, let the supporters know how important their backing would be during the match. Only three members of the Forest team had experience of playing at Wembley. They were Frank Clark, Larry Lloyd and Ian Bowyer. It was Forest's first visit to Wembley since winning the FA Cup in 1959. In another fitting gesture, players from that cup-winning side were invited as the club's guests of honour. But a request for both Clough and his assistant Peter Taylor to lead the Reds out of the Wembley tunnel was turned down.

The Wembley matchday programme, which cost 30p, stated that nothing had seemed beyond the capabilities of Forest so far that season, having taken Division One by storm and making clear their determination to win a trophy. 'Their success this season represents one of the most astonishing transformations of a team in modern football,' declared the programme's Forest profile. There could have been no sweeter way for Clough to reach Wembley than by beating the club that had sacked him after just forty-four days. In the two-legged semi-final against Leeds United, the Reds notched-up a 7-3 aggregate victory. Before that, they had beaten West Ham, Notts County, Aston Villa and Bury, scoring eleven goals in the process; the defence had conceded just two. With goalkeeper Peter Shilton cup-tied, England youth team player Chris Woods deputised in each match despite not having played a League game. The Wembley programme added, 'Clough has harnessed a heady mix of strength, aggression, skill, perception and that undeniable secret to success in all realms of cup-tie football, the "killer" instinct.' It concluded that this appearance at Wembley signalled the dawn of what promised to become the most exciting chapter in Forest's history. The game would also provide a valuable place in the UEFA Cup. The League Cup held a great deal more prestige than it does these days and the fielding of weakened teams was virtually unheard of.

Forest and Liverpool were both making club history for themselves by appearing in their first League Cup Final. Previously, the Merseyside club had not been beyond the fifth round, while Forest had failed to progress past the fourth round. With both sides well known for their red shirts, it was the toss of a coin that decided who would wear red at Wembley. Bob Paisley had been at the City Ground to watch Forest beat Leeds in the semi-final and afterwards Clough's son Nigel spun a coin in the Forest dressing room. Paisley called it wrong and Forest wore their familiar red shirts at Wembley while Liverpool wore white. Clough would later joke that Paisley was exasperated that he could not even win the toss of a coin against Forest.

Liverpool: Clemence, Neal, Smith, Thompson, Kennedy, Hughes, Dalglish, Case, Heighway, McDermott, Callaghan. Sub: Fairclough.
Nottingham Forest: Woods, Anderson, Clark, McGovern, Lloyd, Burns, O'Neill, Bowyer, Withe, Woodcock, Robertson. Sub: O'Hare

Attendance: 100,000

My ticket for the game, for a seat among the Forest fans in the South Terrace, cost £5. The message printed on it stated, 'You are advised to take up your position by 2.30pm.' Before the match, the Central Band of the Royal Air Force played a selection of well-known tunes, including 'The Dambusters' and 'The Entertainer'. Unfortunately, where entertainment is concerned, the action that followed did not always meet that description for many Forest fans who saw their team under the cosh in the second half. There were plenty of anxious moments. The match will largely be remembered for the outstanding performance of Forest's goalkeeper Woods who, at eighteen years and 124 days, was the youngest 'keeper ever to play in a Wembley final. He showed no signs of nerves and coped with everything that came his way, despite playing without wearing gloves. The only time he was beaten was when a shot by Terry McDermott found the back of the net, but an offside decision against Kenny Dalglish meant the 'goal' was disallowed. Forest, who were without first team regulars Shilton, Gemmill and Needham (all cup-tied), as well as the injured Colin Barrett, did a remarkable job at keeping the score goalless. Liverpool, with a number of England internationals in their side, kicked-off and almost scored with their first attack. Dalglish had a golden chance to put his side ahead, but his shot went wide. It seemed that he had been so surprised to have the opportunity that early in the game that he was not composed enough to slot the ball home. Ian Bowyer went close for Forest when his dipping shot went narrowly over the bar.

In the second half, Liverpool stepped-up a gear and put more pressure on Forest. Their midfield did well to cut off Forest's vital supply to John Robertson, but the Merseysiders were largely restricted to long-range efforts. When Liverpool did get close to the Forest goal, more heroics by the young Woods saw him dive bravely at the feet of Dalglish after the ball squirmed away from the 'keeper following a Ray Kennedy effort. Forest suffered a setback when John McGovern had to be substituted due to a groin injury and was replaced in midfield by John O'Hare. There were just seconds of normal time remaining when Forest almost grabbed a winner. Tony Woodcock forced Ray Clemence into making a superb save. Ninety minutes without a goal meant there would be extra time. Clough stayed on the bench rather than going to speak to his players, which was a decision he repeated in the 1991 FA Cup Final. Liverpool brought on 'super sub' David Fairclough to replace Kennedy, who was suffering from a stomach bug, but the stalemate continued until the final whistle. It meant there would have to be a replay a few days later.

All the post-match praise was heaped on Chris Woods and his excellent performance, with one newspaper describing him as 'the eighteen-year-old goalkeeping hero'. According to the same report, when journalists asked to speak to him after the game, Woods 'looked sheepishly out of Forest's dressing room and said, "You want to talk to me? You'd better ask the boss if it's OK"'. After the Leeds semi-final, Woods had asked Clough if it was alright to be interviewed on television. The manager responded, 'Yes, but be careful what you say – I haven't picked the team for Wembley yet.' Once again, Clough allowed his young 'keeper to speak to the media after the Wembley final. 'The only time I felt nervous was when I was waiting before the kick-off with nothing to do,' said Woods. 'But after the first goal kick I felt great. I just wanted to do well and luck was on my side.'

Writing in the *Sunday Mirror*, Ken Jones said, 'When it was all over at Wembley a boy, Chris Woods, had the right to be called a man.' Jones said there were no other contenders for Man of the Match. The Liverpool goalkeeper, Ray Clemence, said his opposite number had been magnificent. 'Nobody doubted the lad's ability, but this was a tremendous test of his temperament and he came through brilliantly,' added Clemence. Bob Paisley commented, 'I thought my lads played well, but so did their young goalkeeper. He was great.' The Forest chairman, Brian Appleby, described it as 'a marvellous Wembley baptism' for Woods. As for Clough, he said of Woods, 'What a tremendous performance to play at Wembley the way he did.' The manager added, 'The lads are a bit tired but I think they'll be OK for Wednesday's replay at Old Trafford.'

32

League Cup Final Replay
Liverpool 0 Nottingham Forest 1
22 March 1978

The more pressure that descends on us this season, the closer our players come together.

A trip to the seaside was the perfect pre-match preparation for Brian Clough's Nottingham Forest as they faced the prospect of a League Cup Final replay at Old Trafford. They now had a second chance to win their first major trophy for nineteen years. The match was arranged for the Wednesday after Saturday's Wembley stalemate. Forest had provisionally agreed to play a League game against Clough's hometown club Middlesbrough at Ayresome Park on the Tuesday, so although that match was rearranged they still went ahead with plans for a short break in Scarborough on the Yorkshire coast. It wasn't all relaxation though, with the Reds using Scarborough's ground for a spot of training in the lead-up to the big rematch. Forest's captain John McGovern stayed behind in Nottingham for treatment after being substituted at Wembley due to a groin injury. He was soon ruled out of contention for the replay and Kenny Burns was skipper for the night.

Once again, John O'Hare was drafted in to replace McGovern and secured a place in the starting line-up. With five first-team regulars out, Forest's stretched resources against the European champions were clear to see when nineteen-year-old striker Stephen Elliott was called-up to be substitute, despite having only appeared in the first team for a County Cup game. Apart from the absence of the cup-tied Graeme Souness, Liverpool were at full strength.

Having closely avoided defeat at Wembley, Forest were determined to make the most of their opportunity. In the replay's match programme (which cost 20p) Clough said it had been 'a great pleasure' to lead his side out at Wembley, before adding, 'and we don't mind being here tonight'. He said the replay was a game that Forest relished, in more ways than one. 'I know it's clogging our fixture list up but we are enjoying the glamour and experience. Apart from anything else we also like and need the money.'

Liverpool: Clemence, Neal, Smith, Thompson, Kennedy, Hughes, Dalglish, Case, Heighway, McDermott, Callaghan. Sub: Fairclough.
Nottingham Forest: Woods, Anderson, Clark, O'Hare, Lloyd, Burns, O'Neill, Bowyer, Withe, Woodcock, Robertson. Sub: Elliott.

Attendance: 54,375

Wearing their yellow away strip, Forest threatened the Liverpool goal early in the game when Frank Clark fed Tony Woodcock, who skipped away from Phil Thompson before crossing for Peter Withe. Although the striker beat Ray Clemence in the air, his header was off-target. I watched the game from a £4 seat high in the stand and behind one of the goals. The action seemed a long way from me but the atmosphere was electric and Forest's yellow shirts were bright and mesmeric under the floodlights. Clough had prepared his players to adopt a more compact approach, with John Robertson tucked into midfield rather than playing out wide, which helped to stifle Liverpool's supply to the dangerous Dalglish. Nevertheless, Woods was called upon to make a fantastic save from a Phil Neal effort and the stalemate continued.

The second half brought the controversial moment for which the replay will be best remembered. In the fifty-second minute a long ball from Frank Clark was nodded down by Withe to Woodcock who delivered a lovely through ball into the path of John O'Hare. As he made his way towards the edge of the Liverpool penalty area, O'Hare found himself in a one-on-one with Clemence and was poised to shoot to break the deadlock and give Forest the lead. But before he could make the match-winning strike, the chasing Phil Thompson cynically brought him down. It was the kind of challenge which, these days, would lead to a red card for the offender. Although television footage showed the foul was outside the area, referee Pat Partridge awarded Forest a penalty. He was surrounded by Liverpool players and it was several minutes before Robertson stepped up to take the spot-kick and slotted the ball perfectly to Clemence's right. Robertson told the press later, 'All I thought about was hitting it as hard as possible and as far away from him as possible.' The headline for the match report in the *Nottingham Evening Post* declared, 'Robbo is Spot-On!' The newspaper's reporter John Lawson named Kenny Burns as his Man of the Match. 'He was impeccably faultless and orchestrated so much of Forest's rhythm from the back,' wrote Lawson. Burns, who as captain received the cup on the pitch, was photographed receiving a hug from Clough as he held the trophy. The Liverpool captain, Emlyn Hughes, described Burns as the outstanding player of the game. 'I thought his performance was out of this world,' he said. But the arguments raged over the penalty decision which led to the match-winning goal. Thompson said he knew he was outside the area when he brought O'Hare down. The Liverpool defender described it as a professional foul. The referee said he was convinced the foul was inside the area. Commented Partridge, 'As far as I was concerned it was a penalty. The television people are entitled to their view but I am going home tonight to have a good night's sleep.' Clough was also asked for his verdict and quipped, 'He was just inside – by about 2 yards! It was a penalty and we stuck it in.' Liverpool were also incensed when, five minutes after the penalty, Terry McDermott had a goal disallowed for handball.

The headline in the *Daily Mirror* hailed 'Cloughie's Wonders!' and reporter Frank McGhee concluded that the controversies and arguments from the match should not sour the achievements of Forest, who he described as 'the team of the season'. McGhee also said there could be no argument about the disallowed goal. Forest had secured a place in the UEFA Cup, but Clough remained firm in the belief that the priority was to win the League Championship and qualify for a place in the European Cup. He said the togetherness of the players would be crucial. 'We've had to deal with any amount of games, injuries, suspensions – you name it,' he said, 'but there is a great feeling of comradeship among the players.'

33

Division One
Coventry City 0 Nottingham Forest 0
22 April 1978

We have gone from the verge of bankruptcy to being the richest club in the country in terms of footballing talent.

When Nottingham Forest won their opening match back in the top flight, Brian Clough invited the legendary former Liverpool boss Bill Shankly into the dressing room. With some of the players still in the bath after the 3-1 win at Everton, Clough called them over to hear what Shankly had to say. 'I'm impressed by what I've just seen,' he told them. 'But the League Championship is a marathon, not a sprint. Remember that and you won't be far away at the end of the season.' Forest's impressive form over the coming months meant they crossed the finish line before the end of the season.

Clough's Reds needed just a point at Coventry City to secure the League title, with another four matches to play. Before the game at City's Highfield Road, only Liverpool could match Forest's points total. Yet the goal difference was so big that it looked extremely unlikely that Forest would be pipped at the post. Clough was determined to make it mathematically certain, so Forest went to Coventry with the aim of at least getting the point that would see them become champions.

Coventry City: Blyth, Roberts, McDonald, Yorath, Holton, Coop, Green, Wallace, Ferguson, Powell, Beck. Sub: Thomson.
Nottingham Forest: Shilton, Anderson, Barrett, O'Hare, Needham, Burns, O'Neill, Bowyer, Withe, Gemmill, Robertson. Sub: Clark

Attendance: 36,881

The reflex save that Peter Shilton made from a Mick Ferguson header will always be remembered as the crucial moment in this match. Forest knew the title must be theirs. In his match report for the *Football Post*, John Lawson described the save as not only 'breathtaking' but 'world-class'. It came in the first half as Coventry piled on the pressure. Most City attacks in the game depended on Ferguson's heading ability. He had already headed the ball down for Ian Wallace to turn quickly and shoot past the post. The big striker also rose to meet a cross from Beck and Shilton held his header on the line. Then came the moment of Shilton brilliance that will live long in the memory of all who witnessed it. Wallace hooked over a cross from the right of the 6-yard box and Shilton was covering his near post. As the ball looped over to Ferguson at the far post, he looked certain to head it powerfully into the net. But Shilton quickly got into position and produced an acrobatic save to palm the ball over the bar. Ferguson sank to his knees in disbelief. Clough often emphasised the importance of having a top class goalkeeper. In Clough's opinion, he was worth eighteen points a season. It could mean the difference between winning a title (or qualifying for Europe) and missing out. In that moment at Highfield Road, it was proven beyond doubt.

Forest attacked at the start of the second half and forced a corner on the left, but it was that man Ferguson who managed to head John Robertson's kick away. Shilton's faultless display continued and near the end of the game he plucked another cross off the head of Ferguson. He then dived to his right to save a shot by Green from just outside the penalty area. Forest twice appealed for a penalty. On the second occasion, Gemmill appeared to be brought down by Coop after good work by Robertson. Although both appeals were turned down, it did not matter. Forest had secured the point they needed to win the title.

The championship trophy was presented before Forest's final home match of the season, against Birmingham City. Clough let members of the local police force hold the trophy as photographs of the team were taken on the pitch. In winning the League, Forest finished seven points ahead of runners-up and European champions Liverpool. The Reds from Nottingham had won twenty-five and lost only three of their forty-two league matches. Clough had now secured the League Championship with two clubs. Not surprisingly, he was named the Manager of the Year, after taking the monthly title four times.

European Cup: First Round, First Leg
Nottingham Forest 2 Liverpool 0
13 September 1978

If we have to meet them sometime – and we probably will – it may as well be now as later.

A managerial masterstroke by Brian Clough helped to inspire Nottingham Forest to a sensational victory over the European champions in this first-round tie. After Liverpool had won the European Cup for the second successive time in May 1978, their manager Bob Paisley admitted that Clough's Forest were the side they would most fear in Europe the following season. But the odds were firmly against the team from Nottingham, who had been looking forward to a trip to somewhere like Spain or Italy to start their European adventure. They had drawn six of their first seven League matches as they defended their championship title, while striker Peter Withe had been sold. A bit of Clough magic was required as Forest faced the European champions. These were the days when the competition really was for 'champions' (not third- or fourth-placed teams) and there were no second chances – it was a knockout situation over two legs. Clough decided to 'front-load' the players' bonuses for the first round, which meant they would get far more for beating Liverpool than any victories later in the competition.

'As far as I was concerned Liverpool were the cream, and if we could "do" them we had a good chance of going all the way,' said Clough in his first autobiography. Although the board of directors questioned the idea of boosting the incentives for the opening round, Clough said he convinced them it made sense to offer the players £1,000 appearance money and £2,000 each to beat Liverpool. He argued that if Forest lost the board would regret not being in a position to pay the impressive bonuses. In an interview with Keith Daniell more than two decades later, Clough admitted the incentives were 'a fortune' at the time, adding, 'I told the board of directors that if they want to beat Liverpool they are going to have to pay.'

The general view of the national press was that Liverpool would win fairly comfortably. One sports writer commented, 'I don't think Forest have the know-how to win the European Cup.' He went on to say that Liverpool had to beat Clough's side if the trophy was to stay in England, before adding, 'Forest are European novices and do not inspire the same awe as Liverpool.' But one journalist who gave Forest a chance was Jeff Powell of the *Daily Mail*. He said it would be 'folly' to write them off completely. He wrote, 'There are niggling fears in the Liverpool camp that this, of all nights, will be the night the wheels fall off their long-running machine.' Powell pointed to the potential impact of twenty-two-year-old Garry Birtles who had played impressively against Arsenal on his Division One debut the previous Saturday. With the player-spotting instinct of Peter Taylor also to be credited, Powell concluded that in buying Birtles for £2,000 from non-league Long Eaton, Clough may have found the bargain of the season.

Forest made one change to the line-up that had just beaten Arsenal 2-1. Archie Gemmill was drafted back into midfield while sixteen-year-old Gary Mills, who had become Forest's youngest ever player in the Football League when he made his debut against the Gunners, was named as a substitute. Garry Birtles was guaranteed his position up front, with Clough declaring publicly, 'The only bloke who is absolutely certain of his place tonight is Garry Birtles.' It would prove to be an unforgettable night for the former carpet-fitter who had been playing reserve team football a few weeks before.

Nottingham Forest: Shilton, Anderson, Barrett, McGovern, Lloyd, Burns, Gemmill, Bowyer, Birtles, Woodcock, Robertson. Subs: Woods, Needham, O'Hare, O'Neill, Mills.
Liverpool: Clemence, Neal, Kennedy (A.), Thompson, Kennedy (R.), Hughes, Dalglish, Case, Heighway, McDermott, Souness. Subs: Ogrozovic, Jones, Hansen, Fairclough, Johnson.

Attendance: 38,316

Birtles scored the first goal and had a big part to play in the second in a momentous win on a sultry, late summer evening at a packed City Ground. The striker showed no fear nor nerves as Liverpool failed to cope with his skills and energy. John Lawson's match report in the *Nottingham Evening Post* described how Birtles and fellow striker Tony Woodcock 'were a constant handful for the Liverpool defence'. Early in the game, Birtles beat defender Phil Thompson with creativity and pace to force Ray Clemence into a reflex save that forced the ball over the bar. The first goal came in the twenty-sixth minute when Ian Bowyer flicked on a ball from Kenny Burns and found Woodcock running through the Liverpool defence. Clemence sensed the danger and came out towards him, only for Woodcock to square the ball to Birtles who side-footed it into an empty net. The City Ground erupted. Television commentator Hugh Johns had already described Birtles' earlier effort as 'explosive'. This time, his infectious enthusiasm was clearly evident as his voice increased in pitch and he declared, 'He's got it – his first ever goal for Nottingham Forest, and it had to be in the European Cup!' That line of commentary was always remembered by my Dad and I when we reflected on Forest's glory years together. We had watched the highlights of the match and Dad loved to repeat that memorable comment in the journalistic style of Hugh Johns. It would always bring the memories flooding back, as it does for me now.

The second goal came towards the end of the game. If the City Ground had had a roof, it would have been lifted off. Left-back Colin Barrett blocked the ball twice just inside the Forest half and it rolled out to Birtles on the left. He beat Thompson again and lifted the ball into the middle of the penalty area. Barrett had continued running and when Woodcock cushioned a header down to the defender he volleyed the ball beautifully into the Liverpool net. Describing the goal, Johns said, 'That was as good as Forest are likely to get all season.' According to Clemence, Liverpool had made the mistake of suddenly treating the game like a one-off domestic match and, in pushing for an equaliser, had 'committed hari-kari'. In *Forest – The 1979 Season*, Clemence described the Liverpool dressing room that night as being like a 'condemned cell' and added that even during his team's Championship celebrations later that season, the memories of this night in Nottingham still haunted them. As Brian Glanville noted in the *Sunday Times*, Forest had exposed Liverpool's deficiencies by running at their defenders.

During the celebrations to mark the unveiling of the Clough statue in Nottingham in 2008, Birtles told me how, after he had put Forest ahead, Phil Thompson had told him, 'One goal won't be enough to take back to Anfield.' After the second went in, the young striker could not help replying as he ran past the Liverpool defender, remarking 'Will two be enough, then?' On reflection, Birtles admitted he was 'out of order' for saying that to a respected England international. But he could not resist it at the time – and two did prove to be enough. John Robertson described Barrett's goal as one of the most important in Forest's history because a 1-0 lead might not have been enough and the Reds' subsequent domination of Europe for two years might never have happened. The next day, even Clough was cautious when he spoke about the return leg at Anfield. He said, 'Liverpool are quite capable of scoring seven goals at home never mind three. I don't know if the two goals will be enough but they certainly satisfied me last night.'

Liverpool boss Bob Paisley admitted his side would face an uphill battle in the second leg. Yet despite throwing everything at Forest during the match at Anfield, they could not score as Clough's side stood firm and battled out a goalless draw. In his match report for the *Nottingham Evening Post*, John Lawson described the Forest players as heroes. He wrote, 'At the end of a deafening, tension-riddled evening at Anfield, Forest manager Brian Clough could not hold back his emotions as he jumped from the dugout to acclaim his team's achievement.' Forest had knocked out the European champions and, according to Clough (reflecting years later), 'struck a mighty blow at Anfield that night'. He said the players had earned their bonuses and secured a psychological advantage. If they could beat Liverpool over two legs, they could beat anyone.

35

Division One
Bolton Wanderers 0 Nottingham Forest 1
25 November 1978

We play the game as most people think it should be played – quick, neat, decisive and clean.

This victory by a single goal on a winter's afternoon at Burnden Park set an incredible record for Brian Clough – a record that lasted more than two decades. His Nottingham Forest side went forty-two consecutive Division One matches without defeat. The Reds' boss described it as his biggest achievement at Forest, despite winning two European Cups. He felt it was so special that he had two silver salvers commissioned, engraved with details of all the games including the results and scorers. He gave one of them to the Forest chairman at the time, Stuart Dryden.

The unbeaten run, which was the equivalent of going a full season without defeat, had started the previous November with a goalless draw at home to West Bromwich Albion. In an interview with Keith Daniell for the DVD *Champions Of Europe – Twenty Five Years On*, Clough spoke of his pride about the record and dismissed criticism from a journalist that it counted less because it had been achieved over two seasons. 'I don't care if it was over twenty-two seasons, it was forty-two games on the trot and we knew we were a good side,' he said.

The line-up for the game against West Brom was Shilton, Anderson, Barrett, McGovern, Lloyd, Burns, O'Neill, Gemmill, Withe, Woodcock and Robertson. Only two players appeared in all forty-two games: Shilton and Robertson. In his autobiography *Super Tramp*, Robertson said the achievement still gave him a huge sense of personal pride. He felt that the players did not receive the wider credit they deserved at the time and the significance of what they achieved was only remembered when Arsenal set a new unbeaten record in the Premier League in 2004.

Clough maintained that all successful sides were built on clean sheets. During the record run, Forest kept twenty-five of them – another source of pride for the master manager. In August 1978, Forest began the defence of their League title with six draws from their opening seven matches. Three of them were goalless. The match before the Bolton game, against Queens Park Rangers, also ended without a goal and prompted Clough to wonder whether the unbeaten run was becoming a burden for the players. He questioned whether their desire to avoid defeat was preventing them playing the free-flowing football for which they had been widely praised. Clough told the *Football Post* that if the impressive run had become a psychological problem for the players, it would be better to be beaten sooner rather than later. May be Forest's injury problems had also begun to catch up with them. Kenny Burns, John McGovern, Martin O'Neill, Colin Barrett and Frank Clark had all missed the match against QPR. Although Ian Bowyer had performed well at left-back while John O'Hare and young Gary Mills worked hard in midfield, Clough knew the Reds needed to stop labouring as they had in that QPR game. For the next match against Bolton, Clark and O'Neill were brought back into the side.

Bolton Wanderers: McDonagh, Nicholson, Walsh, Greaves, Jones, Allardyce, Morgan, Reid, Gowling, Worthington, McNab. Sub: Whatmore.
Nottingham Forest: Shilton, Anderson, Clark, Needham, Lloyd, Bowyer, O'Neill, Gemmill, Birtles, Woodcock, Robertson. Sub: O'Hare

Attendance: 25,692

The Forest players did not have much time to prepare for the game after arriving late at the ground. It was reported that their train did not get into Bolton station until almost twenty-past-two. A quick journey by coach took them to Burnden Park in time to meet the Football League's deadline of half past two for handing in team sheets. When the game got underway, Forest had an early chance to go ahead. Woodcock won a corner on the left and although John Robertson's kick was punched away by Jim McDonagh as David Needham tried to score with a header, Robertson returned the ball and Bowyer had a left-foot shot charged down. But Bolton attacked strongly in response. They had a penalty appeal turned down when the Reds' goalkeeper Peter Shilton and Wanderers' striker Alan Gowling challenged for the ball following a corner. The home side claimed Shilton had pushed the Bolton man, but the referee gave a corner, which was cleared. As half-time approached, Shilton was called into action again, diving to his right to save a Gowling header.

The second half saw the action swing from end-to-end. A shot by Bolton's Peter Reid was deflected wide and seconds later Forest appealed for a penalty when Ian Bowyer was brought down. But the referee awarded the Reds a free-kick on the edge of the penalty area. The breakthrough came in the sixty-fifth minute when the Reds won a free-kick on the left. Robertson curled the ball in with his right foot and several Forest players tried unsuccessfully to make contact. McDonagh was unable to do anything as the ball continued on its way and crept in at the far post. It sealed another victory for the visitors and, more importantly, continued their unbeaten run. Clough was probably even more satisfied with the achievement because the previous record had been held by his former club Leeds United, who had gone thirty-four games without defeat.

The only disappointment for Forest was that big defender Larry Lloyd had to go off injured towards the end of the Bolton game. The win left Forest fourth in Division One, behind West Brom, Everton and leaders Liverpool. Bolton were three places above bottom club Chelsea, who had lost at home to Manchester United.

Forest's unbeaten run came to an end in their next game, when they lost 2-0 to Liverpool at Anfield in December 1978. The record stood until 2004, when Arsenal went forty-three games unbeaten by defeating Blackburn. The Gunners went on to set a new record of forty-nine matches without defeat. It prompted Clough to say Arsenal were as close to perfection as any team he had seen. He told *The Sun*, 'When I watch them I drool – and not because I'm nearly seventy. It's because I see a team who have brought to football the art of simplicity. High technical skills, rhythm, a joy to behold.' Clough said he admired their manager Arsene Wenger and considered him an idol. In response, Wenger said it was good to receive such a compliment and that what Clough had achieved at Forest was incomparable. The Frenchman said it made him proud to hear Clough liked the way Arsenal played football. He went on to say he hoped to match Clough's record of two European Cups, but admitted that to achieve it with Forest's resources had been 'totally surreal in today's terms'.

It was fitting that to mark the twelfth anniversary of Clough's death in September 2016, Arsenal fans joined Forest supporters in applauding in memory of the Master Manager in the twelfth minute of their League Cup tie at the City Ground. Ten years before, Arsenal had donated a special-edition signed shirt to help raise money for Nottingham's Clough statue. The redcurrant shirt, signed by players including Thierry Henry, Robert Pires and Dennis Bergkamp, marked the London club's last season at Highbury. It was auctioned off for more than £400.

In an interview with the BBC shortly before he died, Clough admitted he was disappointed Forest's record had been beaten, as he cherished it more than the European Cups. 'Arsenal are nothing short of incredible,' he said, before joking, 'I'm loathed to confess it, but they could have been nearly as good as us.'

36

League Cup Final
Nottingham Forest 3 Southampton 2
17 March 1979

It was once regarded as the Cinderella competition but not any longer and having won it the previous season, we didn't want to let it go.

Nottingham Forest's preparations for this prestigious match at Wembley were unconventional to say the least. But for Brian Clough, it was simply a way of relaxing the players before a crucial game. The Reds had arrived at a hotel in London the day before the match – nothing unusual about that. But in the evening the players were encouraged to drink as much alcohol as they wanted. Clough ordered a dozen bottles of champagne and insisted that not a drop was left. For those that wanted beer, pints were ordered. Clough and assistant manager Peter Taylor kept the players entertained with funny stories from their past, especially the time they spent at Hartlepool. John Robertson recalls in his autobiography *Super Tramp* that when the pair were in the right mood, even Morecambe and Wise in their heyday could not have entertained them better. Some of the players returned to their rooms a little worse for wear. In his book *My Magic Carpet Ride*, Garry Birtles remembers falling over and crawling on all fours on the way up to his room.

Another surprise before the match got underway was the sight of Taylor leading out the Forest team at the famous old stadium. Officials had previously refused Forest permission for both Clough and Taylor to lead out the team, so it was Taylor who appeared alongside Southampton boss Lawrie McMenemy. The pitch had been cleared of the last remnants of snow but it soon cut up and did not help Forest's neat passing style of football – but perhaps neither did the booze that had been consumed the night before.

Nottingham Forest: Shilton, Barrett, Clark, McGovern, Lloyd, Needham, O'Neill, Gemmill, Birtles, Woodcock, Robertson. Sub: Bowyer.

Southampton: Gennoe, Golac, Peach, Williams, Nicholl, Waldron, Ball, Boyer, Hayes, Holmes, Curran. Sub: Sealy.

Attendance: 100,000

A strong half-time team-talk from Clough was required after a terrible first half for Forest. The Reds won the toss and decided to attack the tunnel end with their thousands of supporters behind Peter Shilton's goal. But it was one of the few things that went right for them before half-time. Southampton's Alan Ball controlled midfield and created the opening goal for full-back David Peach in the sixteenth minute. That increased Southampton's confidence and they nearly went further ahead when Shilton had to stoop down at the feet of Phil Boyer after a cross from former Forest player Terry Curran. For the Reds, Robertson had time and space to cross the ball, but it was too high for O'Neill at the far post. Clough's side had failed to find their rhythm and, 1-0 down at the interval, it was time for him to deliver the warning the players needed to hear.

'Right, you lot, don't go blaming this on last night,' Clough told the players at half-time. John McGovern recalls that the dressing room was not a pleasant place to be at that time. In his autobiography *From Bo'ness to the Bernabeu*, he says the manager told them, 'How dare you underperform with your wives, girlfriends, relations and supporters in the stands.' Recalling the half-time 'discussion' in the book *Forest – the 1979 Season*, McGovern says the players decided it was time to step things up. 'We had to play the ball quicker than we had in the first half,' he said. A transformed Forest were soon on the rampage, with striker Birtles playing a vital role. Having already been catapulted from the obscurity of life in the reserves to European Cup glory virtually overnight, the former carpet-fitter scored two goals and had another two ruled out for offside. Years later, he still felt disappointed not to have celebrated a hat-trick because he was confident one of the disallowed goals should have counted.

For the equaliser, Birtles capitalised on the indecisiveness of Chris Nicholl to shoot high into the roof of the net. In the seventy-seventh minute, the young striker received a pass from Tony Woodcock and beat Nicholl before sliding the new-look red-and-white ball under the advancing Terry Gennoe. Woodcock confirmed his return to goalscoring form by making it 3-1 in the eighty-second minute. Although Nick Holmes got a late goal for Southampton, Forest became the first club to retain the League Cup.

Whether or not Forest's dramatic transformation involved some of the Forest players overcoming the effects of a hangover, the impact of Clough's comments at half-time cannot be underestimated. Writing his match report for the following Monday's *Daily Telegraph*, Donald Saunders said that anyone who doubted the 'hypnotic' effect managers can have on modern footballers needed only to be reminded of the major role Clough played in this cup final. Saunders wrote,

> During the interval, a few well-chosen words from him transformed a witless, dissident team, seemingly tottering towards defeat, into aggressive, conquering heroes and so helped produce the most entertaining Wembley final since Don Rogers and Swindon humbled Arsenal, ten years ago.

Lawrie McMenemy said he was bitterly disappointed and had warned his players not to expect a comfortable second half after dominating the first. 'I knew Brian Clough would gee them up,' he said. According to Robert Oxby of the *Daily Telegraph*, the effect of Clough's words was all too clear before the second half began. 'The evidence was shown in the way the Forest players ran out after the break as if the pitch was a sanctuary from the tongue-lashing they had obviously received,' wrote Oxby.

'We hadn't played,' said Clough afterwards. 'We were just runners in the first half.' Reflecting later on a momentous season, he said he was proud to have created another piece of football history by winning the League Cup for the second successive year. 'It's never been done before – and that's now down in the record books forever.'

37

European Cup Semi-final: First Leg
Nottingham Forest 3 Cologne 3
11 April 1979

The only way Cologne can surprise us tonight is by suddenly producing a Bofors gun or a doodlebug.

Reflecting on his side's success in lifting the European Cup for the first time in 1979, Brian Clough said the highlight for him had been the way they overcame Cologne in the semi-final, not only in the vital second leg, when they needed to score an away goal, but in the first leg at home, when they were trailing 2-0 at one stage. The match at the City Ground was befitting the final itself: action-packed, full of skill and dramatic to the very end.

In the run-up to the first game, Clough had given his star winger John Robertson unlimited leave of absence following the death of his brother in a road accident. The *Daily Mail* reported the day before the big match that Clough had told Robertson to go home to Scotland as soon as possible following news of the car crash. 'I told him he could stay in Scotland or come back and play,' said Clough. 'The decision was left entirely to John – there was nothing else I could do in such tragic circumstances.' Robertson decided to play. In his book he said it would have been what his brother Hughie would have wanted him to do.

Clough described Robertson's inclusion in the side as an important bonus for the team. 'Cologne are typically German – technically good, disciplined, methodical and efficient,' he told the press. 'We need to produce something a little unorthodox to throw at them, and short of playing Peter Shilton at centre forward, John Robertson is our best means of the surprise element.' There was no way, said Clough, that he would be turning Robertson into the most talented full-back in the world. 'If their chap comes galloping forward willy-nilly, we'll tear him apart just like we did with John Gidman against Aston Villa a week ago.' Forest had won that match 4-0. For the Cologne game, they were without Kenny Burns, who had been recovering from injury, the suspended Viv Anderson and the ineligible £1-million man Trevor Francis. Cologne went into the match with their manager Hennes Weisweiller saying his side needed only one away goal. 'Then we can afford to lose narrowly and have the chance of an outright win in Cologne,' he said. The wily Weisweiller got much more than he bargained for.

Nottingham Forest: Shilton, Barrett, Bowyer, McGovern, Lloyd, Needham, O'Neill, Gemmill, Birtles, Woodcock, Robertson. Sub used: Clark
Cologne: Schumacher, Konopka, Zimmermann, Schuster, Gerber, Cullmann, Van Gool, Prestin, Muller, Neumann, Glowacz. Sub used: Okudera.

Attendance: 40,804

On a mudbath of a pitch, Forest seemed to be caught cold and conceded a goal after just six minutes. A low shot from Roger Van Gool eluded Shilton and hit both posts before going in. The visitors doubled their lead after nineteen minutes with a simple tap-in by Dieter Muller. Archie Gemmill suffered an injury and had to leave the field. Frank Clark came on and Ian Bowyer switched from left-back to midfield. Shocked Forest fans thought their team was on the way out, but the players fought back brilliantly. Birtles scored to reduce the deficit with a header. As a former centre forward himself, Clough later reflected on how well Birtles had taken his goal. 'The way he put that header in against Cologne must have brought back memories of Tommy Lawton to the people of this city,' he said. 'It may have seemed as though he had plenty of time but the goal was a lot more difficult than people imagined.'

Bowyer hit an equaliser with a low shot through a crowded penalty area before Robertson put the Reds ahead with a diving header. As he made his way back to the halfway line he thought of his brother and dedicated the goal to him. But Cologne were not finished. Their substitute, a little Japanese forward, Yasuhiko Okudera, shot from 25 yards and the ball squirmed under Shilton then into the net. The inevitable newspaper headline read, 'Japanese Sub Sinks Forest'.

The final score was 3-3 and Clough was impressed with how his side had fought back. He admitted that at 2-0 down, Forest appeared to have had no hope. 'We've been dead and buried before but never quite as deeply as that,' he reflected. 'I don't think any other club side in the world could have hauled themselves up from the grave as we did that night in turning a 2-0 deficit into a 3-2 lead and even though we conceded a late equaliser we knew we had achieved the impossible.'

38

European Cup Semi-final, Second Leg
Cologne 0 Nottingham Forest 1
25 April 1979

As long as we are on our game, the Germans won't know what's hit them.

Brian Clough looked at the lens of the television camera and pulled no punches. 'I hope anybody's not stupid enough to write us off,' he said. Despite Nottingham Forest facing a colossal task in Cologne, with away goals counting double from the 3-3 result of the first leg, Clough was confident his side could win and secure a place in the European Cup Final. They had to go to the huge Mungersdorfer Stadium and either win or get an improbable high-scoring draw (4-4 or better). Most observers wrote off Forest's chances – but not Clough, nor his assistant Peter Taylor.

'We always think we can win,' the Reds' manager told television journalist Gary Newbon. Clough said he had not been overly impressed with Cologne, who had let a two-goal lead slip. 'We're despondent, obviously, not going to Cologne with a lead, but far from out of any competition,' he said. The Germans, on the other hand, believed they were already in the final. They had printed a European Cup Final brochure and organised tickets and buses in anticipation of going to Munich. Posters around the ground advertised the ticket arrangements for the final. 'Talk about putting your towels out on the sunbeds,' commented Garry Birtles in his book. It only served to make Forest even more determined to go through.

Forest's line-up saw the return of Viv Anderson and Kenny Burns in defence, with Frank Clark at left-back. Archie Gemmill and Colin Barrett were both injured and Trevor Francis was still ineligible. Cologne's manager said his side would not sit on their three away goals. 'We shall play our normal game, on the offensive,' said Hennes Weisweiller. 'We have to do, because Forest are likely to score again – so we must.'

Cologne: Schumacher, Konopka, Zimmermann, Strack, Schuster, Cullmann, Van Gool, Glowacz, Muller, Neumann, Prestin. Subs used: Flohe, Okudera.

Nottingham Forest: Shilton, Anderson, Clark, McGovern, Lloyd, Burns, O'Neill, Bowyer, Birtles, Woodcock, Robertson.

Attendance: 60,000

Around 6,000 Forest fans were in the stadium on a damp, cold and misty night. They watched their team soak up some early pressure as Cologne went for the instant kill. The Reds' first serious effort came after fifteen minutes when a fierce volley from Martin O'Neill went wide. Dieter Muller missed a great chance when he shot narrowly wide from around 10 yards, before limping off before half-time. It was a sign that it could be Forest's night.

Keeping a clean sheet was Forest's priority and they were content to let the Germans push forward and catch them on the counter-attack. Ian Bowyer scored the most important goal of his career in the sixty-fifth minute. Garry Birtles flicked on John Robertson's corner at the near post and as the ball reached Bowyer at around chest height he stooped to head it into the roof of the net.

Peter Shilton made a superb save in the last minute, hurling himself to the left to keep out a curling 25-yard rocket from Harald Konopka. Not only did he save it but he also pounced on the rebound to dash Cologne's hopes of an equaliser. After the game, Clough was full of praise for Bowyer, saying he was worth £1 million. The manager was asked at what stage he believed Forest were going to win. He replied, 'In the last ninety seconds. That last quarter of an hour was a hell of a long time.'

The Forest fans were praised for their behaviour in Germany. The club received a letter from the Vice-Consul at the British Consulate-General in Munich. After congratulating the team on its 'magnificent performance', Mr C. Pattinson continued,

> The main reason however for writing this letter is to let you know that Bavarian Radio, on the morning after the match, in their pre-breakfast programme made a special point of emphasising the disciplined behaviour of the Nottingham Forest supporters. After all the adverse criticism of British football supporters, especially when their clubs are playing abroad over the last couple of years, I feel that you and, if possible your supporters, should be informed of this complimentary mention. It doesn't happen very often!

The letter reflected the importance that Clough placed on good behaviour by fans. There was no doubt that he was now relishing the trip to Munich for the final. 'Everything about Germany is right for us,' he said. 'We like the people, we like the towns, we like the football they play.'

39

European Cup Final
Malmo 0 Nottingham Forest 1
30 May 1979

This is an unbelievable milestone in my life.

Brian Clough arrived in Munich feeling relaxed, having just completed a family holiday in Crete. He looked tanned and confident and even managed to fit in a game of squash on the morning of the European Cup Final. But he had faced one of the toughest tasks in his managerial career: telling two players they would not being playing in this vital match, the climax of the season and possibly their careers. Four players were, in effect, battling for two places.

Trevor Francis' place was virtually guaranteed. He had scored the winner in the final League match of the season against West Brom and again in a 3-1 victory against Mansfield Town in the County Cup Final just a week before the Munich showpiece. When Clough asked Archie Gemmill and Martin O'Neill whether they were both fit, they both replied they were. 'Well, I'm absolutely delighted – because neither of you are playing,' said Clough. Despite their best efforts to get fit, Clough felt they were not ready and chose Frank Clark to slot in at left-back, allowing Ian Bowyer to play in midfield.

Years later, Clough reflected on the difficult situation he had faced in delivering the bad news to two of his star players. He said, 'It's not easy to tell a guy who you are very close to for nine months – you look on them as sons – that they're not playing in the pinnacle of their football career, the European Cup.' But that was all part and parcel of management.

There was a slightly tense atmosphere on the team coach as they made their way to the Olympic Stadium. But that quickly changed thanks to an unsuspecting German. The police outriders had attracted the attention of some fans to the coach. As two young men looked across and pointed out the players, one was so engrossed that he walked into a lamp post. The atmosphere on the bus was instantly lifted and the laughing and joking began. In their book *The Big Matches*, Brian Moore and Martin Tyler wrote, 'The spell was broken. And who knows, that young German with the sore head might well have played an important role in the events of the night…'

Malmo: Moller, R. Andersson, M. Andersson, Jonsson, Erlandsson, Prytz, Tapper, Ljungberg, Kinnvall, Hansson, Cervin. Subs used: Malmberg, T. Andersson.
Nottingham Forest: Shilton, Anderson, Clark, McGovern, Lloyd, Burns, Francis, Bowyer, Birtles, Woodcock, Robertson.

Attendance: 57,500

Six years after being knocked out of the European Cup at the semi-final stage with Derby County, Clough and his assistant Peter Taylor were, at last, watching their Forest team in the final. But the match was something of an anticlimax. Malmo, who had been written off by many football experts, played a mainly cautious game and were happy to keep behind the ball and stifle the Forest threat for most of the first half. With little more than injury time remaining before the break, the Reds scored the winning goal.

Ian Bowyer found John Robertson, who was being marked down the left by two players. He shimmied one way and then the other, before creating a little bit of space for a cross that landed at the far post. Francis showed the electric pace that had frightened Malmo throughout the half and got his head to the ball and scored. It was a magical moment. Clough had a photograph of it put on his wall. He said it had been a good goal, considering Malmo had most of their players back defending. 'It was the feet of a genius called John Robertson and somebody's head called Trevor Francis – who they said I'd paid too much money for. He won the European Cup Final.'

Among the 20,000 Forest fans who had made their way to Germany was the future chairman of the supporters' club, Paul Ellis. He said that while it had been a fairly boring match, one piece of real quality got the vital goal. 'We looked to our left as the ball was whipped across by Robertson and there was Francis – absolutely fantastic. Our fans completely filled the whole of one end of the stadium with their flags and scarves and I felt proud to see it. I'd supported Forest since 1958 and never expected the club to reach such heights. Back then we really were a small club and I didn't think we would win very much, especially after we were relegated. The first few years under Clough were incredible. You had to pinch yourself when you thought about what Forest achieved.'

After the final whistle, Clough gave a familiar salute, his forefinger and thumb forming a circle in the air. As he entered the post-match press conference, he was clearly surprised by the size and formality of it, with desks, microphones, lights and around 200 writers. He first words were: 'Are we on bl**dy trial or something?' The sense of anticlimax continued in the dressing room. It was empty within half an hour. Some players met their wives; others went to celebrate in a club. But there was nothing extravagant. Brian Moore and Martin Tyler concluded in their book that the 1970s belonged to one man: Brian Clough. His last words to the players after the final came when he popped his head around the dressing-room door. 'What a great way to finish a season,' he said. 'Thanks a lot – I'm off.'

40

European Super Cup
Barcelona 1 Nottingham Forest 1
(Forest win 2-1 on aggregate)
5 February 1980

Even their name has got a bit of a glamorous ring about it.

Nottingham Forest's glamourous fixture with Barcelona was described by Brian Clough as a milestone for his club. But it appeared that many Forest fans needed convincing that this clash of the European giants was really worthwhile watching. The day before the first leg at the City Ground, the Reds had sold fewer than half of their 14,000 seat tickets at £4 each. That may not seem a lot of money compared with today's prices, but you have to remember that in the days of Forest's European adventure a loaf of Mothers Pride bread was 26p and a can of Heinz baked beans was 15p.

Forest's assistant secretary, Paul White, told the *Nottingham Evening Post* that he could appreciate why there were so many spare tickets. He said the team had enjoyed a spate of big matches recently, including two big cup games against Liverpool in less than a week, and it had hit people hard in the pocket. Still to come was a European Cup tie against Dynamo Berlin and the return League Cup tie against Liverpool. White also stressed the importance of the two-legged fixture against the Cup Winners' Cup holders, Barcelona. He said UEFA treated the competition as seriously as the European Cup, so the Super Cup was 'anything but a glorified friendly match'.

Clough's frustration at Forest's 2-0 FA Cup defeat by Liverpool just days before the first leg led to an outburst in which he said he wanted the Reds to beat Barcelona 'so comprehensively that they have to invite me to manage them'. He added that he would love to manage a club like Barcelona, but a report in the local newspaper stated that his comments would be viewed as 'primarily gate-boosting propaganda' ahead of the City Ground match. That game, in front of nearly 24,000 spectators and played on a muddy and heavy pitch, ended in a 1-0 win for Forest. The eleventh-minute goal came from Charlie George, who was making his City Ground debut while on loan from Southampton for a month. Despite the slender lead, Clough was confident his side could win the Super Cup when they went to the magnificent Camp Nou, where there would be nearly four times as many spectators. 'We can beat Barcelona over there,' said the Reds' boss. 'It will be a delight to knock the ball about and show our flair on a good pitch.' The only change to the Forest side from the first leg was the recall of John McGovern, which meant Martin O'Neill would be on the bench. Clough thanked the managers of England and Scotland, Ron Greenwood and Jock Stein, for releasing five of his players from international duty. The day before the game, in typical Clough style, Forest trained and relaxed on the beach in the warm Spanish sunshine.

Barcelona: Artola, Estella, Migueli, Olmo, Serrat, Rubio, Simonsen, Sanchez, Roberto, Asensi, Carrasco. Sub used: Esteban
Nottingham Forest: Shilton, Anderson, Gray, McGovern, Lloyd, Burns, Francis, Bowles, Birtles, George, Robertson. Sub used: O'Neill.

Attendance: 90,000

Both sides had goals disallowed in the opening ten minutes. Garry Birtles hit the back of the net first, but Trevor Francis was penalised for handball. Then the former European Footballer of the Year, Alan Simonsen, had a goal ruled out due to a foul on Peter Shilton. Simonsen was the home team's greatest threat and won a penalty in the first half-hour. The spot-kick was dispatched by Roberto and the honours were now even. Trevor Frecknall in the *Nottingham Evening Post* reported, 'The pride of two giants was at stake; and to their credit, they overcame the tension that poured down three tiers of seating and provided a contest that contained more skill than bite.'

The Forest defence stood firm and John Robertson was described as threatening to shred the right side of the Barcelona defence. Stan Bowles' work rate and skill in midfield was said to be a 'revelation' while John McGovern was as tenacious as ever. The Reds went 2-1 ahead on aggregate just before half-time. Larry Lloyd beat goalkeeper Artola to the ball and nodded it on to Kenny Burns, whose quick reactions helped him plant a header firmly into the net. There was a collectors' item early in the second half: Robertson missed a penalty. Bowles had been tripped just inside the penalty area by Olmo, but Robertson's spot-kick was parried by the goalkeeper and quickly cleared. The *Nottingham Evening Post* said there seemed little doubt that Artola had moved before the kick was taken.

There was an injury blow for the Reds when Trevor Francis had to be replaced by O'Neill due to a badly gashed leg – Francis needed six stitches and missed the next two matches. Peter Shilton denied Simonsen a number of times to ensure Forest kept their overall lead and won the cup – well, it was not a cup as such; it was actually a large plaque. But that did not matter to Forest. While England's cricketers were losing by eight wickets in the third Ashes Test in Melbourne, despite an unbeaten century by Ian Botham, Britain could proudly boast the home of football's European Super Cup winners.

41

European Cup Final
Hamburg 0 Nottingham Forest 1
28 May 1980

It was a case of get your shorts on and into your flip-flops and down to the beach.

The preparations for Nottingham Forest's second successive European Cup Final were typical of Brian Clough: they spent a week relaxing in the Spanish sunshine. There was a little training too, for example the occasional run along the beach, while Peter Shilton found a traffic island on which to practise with trainer Jimmy Gordon. But Clough's emphasis was on recharging the batteries by taking things easy after a long season, at the end of which the Reds had finished fifth in Division One. After losing the final of the League Cup, the only way they would qualify to play in Europe the following season was by winning the European Cup. Having enjoyed a break in the sunshine, Clough knew that when the players next saw a football, at the impressive Bernabeu Stadium in Madrid, they would welcome it like a long-lost friend.

Forest had reached the final by beating the likes of Dynamo Berlin and Ajax along the way, but found themselves the underdogs despite being the holders. They were without the injured Trevor Francis who had snapped an Achilles tendon earlier in the month. With only one recognised striker, Garry Birtles, Clough and his assistant Peter Taylor brought in seventeen-year-old Gary Mills as part of a five-man midfield. Hamburg had German internationals Manny Kaltz and Felix Magath, while England's Kevin Keegan was their main attacking threat. Larry Lloyd and Kenny Burns made sure he did not have an enjoyable game.

Interviewed before the match, Clough was asked how Forest would cope with the skill of Kaltz. He replied, 'We've got a little fat guy, a very talented, highly skilled, unbelievable outside left. He'll turn him inside out.' Clough was referring warmly to John Robertson, who he later described as 'the Picasso of our game'. The manager would often have a gentle joke about Robbo's appearance, but Clough recognised the importance of the skilful winger, who would create another moment of magic to win the European Cup.

Hamburg: Kargus, Kaltz, Nogly, Jakobs, Buljan, Hieronymous, Keegan, Memering, Milewski, Magath, Reimann. Sub used: Hrubesch.
Nottingham Forest: Shilton, Anderson, Gray, McGovern, Lloyd, Burns, O'Neill, Bowyer, Birtles, Mills, Robertson. Subs used: O'Hare, Gunn.

Attendance: 50,000

Clough described it as one of those moments when you knew something special was about to happen. Twenty minutes into the match, Robertson received the ball on the left. He jinked between two defenders and played a one-two with Birtles, who just managed to return the ball under pressure. The winger took the ball off the foot of Keegan and struck a right-foot shot from the edge of the penalty area. The ball went in off the inside of the post and Robertson stood there, triumphantly, with both arms in the air as he was mobbed by his teammates.

Forest came under immediate pressure from the restart. Willi Reimann had the ball in the net after a long-range shot from Kaltz, but it was disallowed because Keegan was offside. More than half an hour had gone by when a save by Shilton was described by television commentator Brian Moore as a magnificent piece of goalkeeping. Keegan chested down a long ball for Milewski to volley at the Forest goal, but Shilton's athleticism allowed him to quickly turn and leap to the left to push the ball away.

For the second half, Hamburg brought on their big striker Horst Hrubesch, but Larry Lloyd and Kenny Burns dealt brilliantly with the aerial threat. After sixty-five minutes Gary Mills tried to relieve the pressure by running 50 yards with the ball, but was eventually forced wide and his shot flew into the Forest fans behind the Hamburg goal. Moments later, Shilton was beaten at last – but Kaltz's 25-yard screamer hammered the post and went out for a goal kick. There was yet more danger for Forest when Nogly tried a shot from 30 yards, but Shilton dived to his left to make another amazing save. On sixty-eight minutes, Clough sent on the experienced John O'Hare to replace young Mills. Towards the end, Frank Gray had to come off injured and was replaced by Bryn Gunn.

Forest could have made it 2-0 in the final few minutes. Birtles, who had carried out his role as the lone striker so well, broke away with the ball. He was left one-on-one with the last defender, Nogly. The Forest centre forward, who had run tirelessly throughout the match and now had his socks around his ankles, nutmegged Nogly and was about to shoot when Kaltz got back in the nick of time and robbed him. The final whistle went soon afterwards. In the foreword of Birtles' book, Clough's son Nigel described how the striker was his hero and said that his performance in this final had left a lasting impression on him. Brian described all his players as heroes that night.

'We had application, tenacity, dedication and pride – you name a good quality and we showed it in every department,' said Clough. He admitted to being 'a bit choked' at the end. Accompanied by Peter Taylor, he went back to an empty dressing room. 'It was an emotional, satisfying moment for us both after the season's slog,' he said. Afterwards, Clough went back out to applaud the thousands of Forest fans who had made the trip to Madrid, only to be left in the dark when the officials turned off the floodlights. Nevertheless, he said he had been glowing so much with pride and pleasure they could have seen him in Barcelona.

42

UEFA Cup Semi-final: Second Leg
Anderlecht 3 Nottingham Forest 0
25 April 1984

I was a bit worried when I saw which country [the referee] came from.

The bitter disappointment that Brian Clough felt after this crucial cup-tie defeat was still evident long after the final whistle. In a BBC local radio phone-in more than ten years later, his opinions about the game were as strong as ever. 'It's a match we could and should have won,' he told a listener. Some dubious refereeing decisions certainly cast doubt about the validity of the final score that saw Clough's Nottingham Forest knocked out of the UEFA Cup when they were so close to reaching the final. It later emerged that the referee had received a substantial loan from the Reds' opponents, Anderlecht.

On their way to reaching the UEFA Cup semi-final, Forest had secured a memorable victory over Celtic in the third round. The home leg against the Scottish club, in front of a crowd of more than 34,000, ended goalless. In Glasgow, a managerial masterstroke by Clough helped the Reds to victory. He took the players to the pub owned by Celtic manager David Hay to enjoy a drink the day before the match. It sent out a clear message to the opposition that the English visitors would not be intimidated by a stadium full of noisy, passionate Scots. Nearly 67,000 spectators watched Forest win the match 2-1 with goals from Steve Hodge and Colin Walsh. A 2-1 aggregate win over Austrian side Sturm Graz brought Clough's men face-to-face with the defending champions, Anderlecht. Two more goals from Hodge, in the last five minutes of the first leg at the City Ground, gave Forest a two-goal advantage going into the away leg.

Forest fans travelling to Belgium had a range of options to choose from, depending on their budget. For those wanting to let the train take the strain, the club ran a *Forest Rail* special that left Nottingham the night before the match and arrived in Brussels on the afternoon of the game. The cost, including a match ticket and insurance, was £44. A slightly cheaper alternative was offered by skills coaches, who advertised a 'high value tour', including a terrace ticket along with coach and ferry charges, for £39.50. But those wanting to push the boat out and fly there (forgive the transport pun) could have a one-day round trip including match ticket and insurance for £104. Add an overnight stay in a top hotel and the cost was £130. The advert by Neilson Travel stated, 'All flights by jet from East Midlands Airport. All hotels first class.' For those who stayed at home and preferred to watch television, there was slapstick comedy on the Wednesday night *Benny Hill Show* on ITV. But the supporters who made the trip to Belgium experienced their own farce as many questioned a penalty decision and a disallowed goal.

Clough decided to leave fit-again Garry Birtles on the bench although he had recovered from a back problem. The striker had not played for more than three weeks and the manager was concerned that while the side needed his experience, he might run out of steam late in the game. In goal, Hans van Breukelen played despite suffering a broken finger in the previous match against Birmingham City. Clough had described the Dutch goalkeeper as a 'dream signing'. Three months before this match, the manager had reflected, 'The only thing I'd bought from Holland before [signing van Breukelen] was cheese and I wasn't that happy about the Dutch because during the Second World War, they were letting the Germans into my backyard at Middlesbrough! But Ronnie Fenton, Liam O'Kane, Alan Hill and myself all went to Holland at various times to see Hans van Breukelen and decided we had come up with a winner.'

Speaking shortly before this second leg, Clough warned that Forest could not afford to sit back and defend for the entire game. He told the *Nottingham Evening Post*, 'I don't honestly think we are capable of keeping them at arm's length for that long. That's proved by the fact we have conceded five goals in our last five matches.' He also said he was concerned that the referee was Guruceta Muro from Spain. 'I was a bit worried when I saw which country he came from,' said Clough. 'I wouldn't say we are exactly on friendly terms with Spain; every time we have gone there for pre-season friendlies, we have had players sent off for absolutely nothing.' Although Forest avoided a red card, Clough would later regret his comments. In theory, Forest were just ninety minutes from reaching a momentous European final. In reality, they faced a controversial exit from the competition.

Anderlecht: Munaron, Grun, De Greef, Czerniatinski, De Groote, Scifo, Vandereycken, Hofkens, Vandenbergh, Olsen, Brylle. Subs: Vekeman, Gudjohnsen, Vercauteren, Hansen, Anderson.
Nottingham Forest: Van Breukelen, Anderson, Swain, Fairclough, Hart, Bowyer, Wigley, Mills, Davenport, Hodge, Walsh. Sub: Sutton, Birtles, Wallace, Thijssen, Gunn.

Attendance: 38,000

The headline in the *Nottingham Evening Post* declared, 'Forest Out – and Furious'. Duncan Hamilton's match report reflected that the Reds had 'filed solemnly away from the Astrid Park Stadium believing they should have reached the UEFA Cup final'. While the players rarely complained about decisions by the officials, they had been left bewildered by the referee's decision to disallow a late Paul Hart header that would have been enough to take them into an all-British final against Spurs. With Forest trailing 3-0 on the night, and 3-2 on aggregate, that header would have taken Forest through on the away-goals rule. In the last minute, Hart had nodded a Gary Mills corner into the net, only for Muro to disallow it for an alleged foul. Afterwards, Hart said he could not understand how the decision had been made and the vital goal ruled out.

Forest's feeling of injustice had already been established when Muro awarded the home side a highly questionable penalty in the fifty-eighth minute. Kenneth Brylle fell in the area, apparently due to a Kenny Swain foul. In his autobiography *My Magic Carpet Ride*, Garry Birtles, who was still on the bench, said Swain was nowhere near the player and the decision was a total travesty. 'There was complete daylight between him and the Anderlecht player he was supposed to have brought down,' he said. Brylle took the spot-kick to put Anderlecht 2-0 up on the night. Hamilton's report makes it clear that Forest were completely overwhelmed by the Belgians who played brilliantly. But the question marks over those two decisive incidents left a nasty taste. In particular, there was a big question mark over the referee's handling of the game. Hans Van Breukelen said it had been 'hard to play against twelve men'. But it seems Clough had smelt something fishy before kick-off. Birtles reveals in his book that, unusually, the Forest boss had kept the dressing-room door open that night so he could keep a lookout. He thought it was strange to see people going in and out of the referee's room on the opposite side of the corridor. Years later, Clough was proved correct in his suspicions that all was not quite right that night.

In 1997, Anderlecht admitted to having paid the referee £18,000 as a loan before the game. UEFA punished the club with a season's ban from European competition. But that was no consolation for the Forest players who felt cheated out of the opportunity of winning a European medal. A bid for financial compensation was unsuccessful. There can be no doubt that, along with fixtures like Derby's bitter defeat to Juventus in the European Cup and Leeds United's bust-up with Liverpool in the 1974 Charity Shield, this is one of the most controversial matches Clough was ever involved in. Reflecting on his fifteenth anniversary at Forest, an article in the club's matchday programme against Liverpool on New Year's Day 1990 suggested that among the disappointments that had accompanied his many glories at Forest, probably the most hurtful was the defeat at Anderlecht. Clough went on to describe Hart's header as one of the most legitimate goals he had seen in thirty years. He still did not understand why it had been ruled out. Nevertheless, it appeared he blamed himself for contributing to what happened. He admitted, 'I knew I had dropped a clanger the day before the game. I was lured by journalists into talking about a Spanish referee and giving them "a line" for a story. It might have done them a favour but it didn't do us much good.' Clough concluded that we all make mistakes and we all learn from them. That was a big admission from someone who was (nearly) always right.

Littlewoods Cup Quarter-final
Nottingham Forest 5 Queens Park Rangers 2
18 January 1989

The players need my apologies more than anybody else...

As Brian Clough made his way down the tunnel after this match, he knew he had probably made a big mistake. His Nottingham Forest team had just sealed an impressive victory to reach the Littlewoods Cup semi-final. The Reds were halfway through ten successive league and cup victories. Yet it was events after the final whistle of this midweek game at the City Ground that would grab all the headlines. Clough's behaviour as the teams left the field would lead to him offering his resignation as Forest manager.

It was midway through the season and Forest were still bidding to make Wembley cup final appearances on three fronts: the FA Cup, the Simod Cup and this competition. They had reached the quarter-final stage of the Littlewoods Cup after beating three 'Cities' (Chester, Coventry and Leicester), scoring fifteen goals along the way. After a 10-0 aggregate win over Chester, Forest won a five-goal thriller against Coventry before meeting David Pleat's Leicester. The Reds held out for a goalless draw against the Foxes, despite having skipper Stuart Pearce sent off shortly after half-time. In the replay at the City Ground, Nigel Clough and Lee Chapman scored in a 2-1 victory. When Forest continued their cup progress with more goals against Queens Park Rangers, some fans could not contain their enthusiasm, leading to the controversial incident involving Clough – and captured by the television cameras.

Nottingham Forest: Sutton, Laws, Pearce, Chettle, Wilson, Hodge, Carr, Webb, Clough, Chapman, Parker. Subs: Crosby, Starbuck.
Queens Park Rangers: Seaman, Ardiles, Pizanti, Parker, Law, Maddix, Stein, Barker, Fereday, Coney, Kerslake. Subs: B. Allen, Herrera.

Attendance: 24,065

Four goals by Lee Chapman, including a first-half hat-trick, guided Forest to victory. The tall striker's first goal was a looping header after Steve Chettle had flicked on a corner. His hat-trick goal was a brilliant right-foot shot; it was the first time in his career that he had scored four goals in a match. Chapman had joined Forest earlier in the season after a disappointing spell at French club Niort. After his impressive performance against QPR he said, 'I was sure at the time I came to Forest from Niort that I was making the right decision ... and I'm doubly sure now.' His four-goal haul also earned him a £500 cheque to give to charity. The other Forest goal was a Nigel Clough penalty. For QPR, the Argentinian World Cup star Ossie Ardiles had to be substituted in the first half due to injury. But by half-time, the game was really all over as Forest led 4-1. The Reds supporters were singing 'Wembley, Wembley' and some could not resist going onto the pitch after the final whistle.

As the players made their way towards the tunnel, Clough was incensed to see some fans on the pitch and he lashed out at several of them. On the gantry above, the television camera was still filming and recorded what happened. One fan who was hit by Clough appeared to be startled when he looked round and realised who had just clobbered him. In his first autobiography, Clough said his wrist was hurting so much after the incident that he needed treatment from the club's physio when he returned to the dressing room. Knowing he was in hot water, the manager offered to resign three times. The club not only turned him down but the chairman, Maurice Roworth, gave Clough his full backing. In a message to supporters, Roworth said he hoped it would make fans think twice before encroaching onto the pitch again. 'Let's face it,' he said, 'that area is our shop floor. It's where the players go about their work and you don't see people invading shops, offices and factories, do you? It's particularly sad for us because the record of behaviour at the City Ground – for which Brian takes great credit – has been almost exemplary over the last fifteen years.' The chairman went on to say that Clough had always been an ambassador for discipline, not only in football but life in general, and that his motives after the match had been good ones. He said judging by the mail he had received, the British public thought the same. There had been around 400 letters in support of Clough's actions and around thirty against them. Roworth also stressed that young people still admired the controversial manager. Within days of the QPR incident, the chairman had received a letter from a talented youngster on Merseyside. He did not want to play for Liverpool or Everton, but was desperate for a trial with Nottingham Forest and Brian Clough.

Clough said his actions had been regrettable but he had been trying to prevent confrontation between fans. The man in charge of policing football in Nottingham, Chief Superintendent Mike Holford, welcomed Clough's expression of regret. 'It is a big man who can apologise later and admit his mistake,' he said. A police spokesman said later that several young supporters had been interviewed and none wished the police to take any action. Clough later described the whole episode as a 'mini crisis' but he helped to defuse the situation by using the same medium that had caught him red-handed in the first place: television. In front of a local TV crew, he met two of the supporters he had confronted. They kissed and made up, quite literally, with the Forest boss offering his cheek so they could give it a conciliatory peck. It was classic Clough.

The local media asked people for their opinions on what had happened after the match. A phone-in poll by BBC Radio Nottingham gave the manager a big thumbs-up. It was reported that in twenty minutes, hundreds of people had called, with just over 80 per cent backing him. A telephone poll by TV-AM had around two-thirds of callers supporting the manager's behaviour. A Forest spokesman told the press that they had received scores of phone calls, with 90 per cent in support. A businessman from Newcastle called to say that if every manager acted that way, the game would be cleaned up very quickly. There were also supportive calls from two school head teachers. But not everyone shared the view that Clough had behaved correctly. A Coventry engineering firm contacted the club to say they were cancelling a major contract with the electricity board because Clough appeared in their adverts. You can only imagine what the sponsors, Littlewoods, thought about it all. In the match programme for the semi-final against Bristol City, they placed an advert that declared their aims in supporting the competition. There was no mention of the previous incident. The full-page advert included the following comment: 'We continue to see our latest challenge as playing a part in making football a family occasion at clubs throughout the country and making football grounds happier places to visit.' The opinions of readers of the *Nottingham Evening Post* appeared to be split, with just over half of the letters supporting Clough. A former Nottinghamshire police inspector wrote to say he admired the Forest boss. He said that while he may have gone 'over the top' in the after-match incident, he agreed with Clough's attempts at tackling the general issue of football hooliganism. Another correspondent felt that Clough's actions had done nothing to enhance the reputation of the club, yet another wrote, 'What's the matter with the world? As seen on TV, Brian Clough did the right thing against the youths who invaded the pitch after the match.'

The Football Association took decisive action and charged Clough with bringing the game into disrepute. However, he appreciated that the FA held the disciplinary hearing at the City Ground rather than in London. Clough was fined £5,000 and received a three-month touchline ban. It meant he had to watch several matches from the directors' box. When Forest faced Queens Park Rangers again for a league match the following month, he said he was aiming for the same result, but added, 'I hope the match is less eventful.' In the matchday programme, he had a message for the club's fans: 'What I would like to say is that I have had tremendous support over the last few weeks from genuine Forest supporters – and that has meant a great deal to me.' Those same fans also received a warning from the Football Association. In the Forest matchday programme for the semi-final against Bristol City there was a 'Notice to Spectators' from the General Secretary of the FA, Ted Croker. Referring to what happened previously, it concluded 'spectators are warned that a repetition of misconduct may result in the closing of the ground'.

Some weeks after the controversial post-match incident, Clough was named the Barclays Manager of the Month for February. Yet his pleasure at receiving the award was tainted by his regret at what had happened on 18 January. He felt he and the team had deserved the award for the previous month too. 'Forest supporters won't need me to tell them that we won all eight games during the month,' he said, 'but because I overstayed my welcome on the pitch during our Littlewoods Cup victory over Queens Park Rangers, it influenced the voting.' Clough was also full of praise for the players and his backroom staff for how they reacted so positively for the match that followed the QPR game. In roundly beating Aston Villa 4-0 at home, Clough was pleased that his side had won convincingly despite the turmoil surrounding the club. He told the *Nottingham Evening Post* that he even disrupted his post-match routine to congratulate nineteen-year-old Terry Wilson on his performance against Villa. 'I got out of the bath to come back into the dressing room and tell him he was incredible,' said Clough. Then he joked: 'We have got a quiet week now.'

44

League Cup Final
Luton Town 1 Nottingham Forest 3
9 April 1989

Everyone will be delighted with the result because we did it in style.

This victory at Wembley marked a major achievement for Brian Clough. By guiding Nottingham Forest to their first major trophy in nine years, Clough had shown he could create a successful and talented team without Peter Taylor. He was assembling an exciting young squad bursting with homegrown talent and clever signings. In his final few seasons at Forest, Wembley almost became the Reds' second home. The manager would joke that the team coach knew its own way there.

Forest's League Cup run had seen victories over Chester City, Coventry City, Leicester City and Queens Park Rangers before a two-legged semi-final against Bristol City. Clough had stated he did not want to experience a hat-trick of semi-final defeats after losing to Anderlecht in the UEFA Cup in 1984 and then to Liverpool in the FA Cup semi-final in 1988. After a 1-1 draw at the City Ground, Forest beat Bristol City 1-0 in the second leg.

Before the final, Clough told the *Nottingham Evening Post* that he was not going to Wembley to simply smile and wave. He said he was going there to get a result against the League Cup holders. Although many people had written off Luton Town, who were languishing third from bottom of Division One, Clough pointed out that his Forest side had not managed to score against them at the City Ground earlier in the season. He was also wary that Luton had benefited from a full week without a game before the Sunday afternoon final, while Forest had played a midweek match against Norwich.

Clough chose Brian Laws to play at right-back against Luton, despite the defender having thirty-six stitches in his hand after an accident involving some glasses he was putting away in a cupboard at home. On the Thursday before the game, the manager threw him a ball and told him to try to take a throw-in. When Laws succeeded with the task, Clough told him he was playing. Laws wore a skin-coloured bandage and later said the adrenalin of playing at Wembley had helped him forget the pain.

Luton Town: Sealey, Breacker, Grimes, Preece, Foster, Beaumont, Wilson, Wegerle, Harford, Hill, Black. Subs: McDonough, Meade.
Nottingham Forest: Sutton, Laws, Pearce, Walker, Wilson, Hodge, Gaynor, Webb, Clough, Chapman, Parker. Subs: Chettle, Glover.

Attendance: 76,130

Clough walked out of the players' tunnel wearing a smart Forest blazer. After both sides had been introduced to the dignitaries, he disappeared down the tunnel that lead to the Royal Box and changed into his favourite 'working clothes': a green sweatshirt. Despite some excellent creative play from his son Nigel during the first half, Forest went behind in the thirty-sixth minute. A Luton corner was headed away by Lee Chapman, but Danny Wilson collected the ball and sent in a cross from the right that was headed home by Mick Harford.

Forest fought back strongly after the break. Ten minutes into the second half a lovely through-ball from Neil Webb went to Steve Hodge, who was brought down in the penalty area by Luton goalkeeper Les Sealey. Nigel Clough kept his cool to equalise with the resulting penalty. The Reds took the lead in the sixty-ninth minute when Webb slotted the ball past Sealey from a cross by Tommy Gaynor. The match was put beyond Luton's grasp when Clough made it 3-1 in the seventy-seventh minute, again from a Gaynor cross.

At the final whistle, Brian Clough gave his Luton counterpart Ray Harford a kiss on the cheek. The Forest boss did not hang around to see Stuart Pearce collect the trophy. He marched towards the Forest fans and paused at the mouth of the players' tunnel to salute them. He said later that he wanted to ensure the players were the focus of the celebrations. 'The players were the ones that earned the glory,' he said. 'I just sit around and shout occasionally and get into trouble.' It was a memorable day for the Clough family because Nigel also collected the Man of the Match award. His Dad insisted that the players report for training the morning after the victory. It was his way of ensuring they did not get carried away by their Wembley win. Later that month they were back at the Twin Towers to win the Simod Cup against Everton. His Forest squad finished third in Division One for the second successive season, while he collected the Manager of the Month award for April. No wonder the headline in the *Football Post* on Saturday 6 May 1989 was 'Top Boss!'

45

FA Cup Semi-final (abandoned)
Liverpool 0 Nottingham Forest 0
15 April 1989

It started as just another, pleasant spring Saturday.

What should have been a momentous match played in glorious sunshine will always be remembered for the most tragic of reasons. This will forever be known as the Hillsborough Disaster. Ninety-six Liverpool fans died following a crush in the Leppings Lane end of Sheffield Wednesday's Hillsborough Stadium. Comments by Brian Clough, for which he later apologised, also caused controversy. He stressed later that he had been misinformed about the circumstances surrounding the terrible events of that afternoon.

In the match programme, Sheffield Wednesday's chairman, Mr H. E. McGee, had a welcome message for both sets of fans, who were returning for their second consecutive FA Cup semi-final. It was a message that would, with hindsight, be looked upon as highly unfortunate. 'As you look around Hillsborough you will appreciate why it has been regarded for so long as the perfect venue for all kinds of important matches,' he wrote, before listing the types of games the stadium had hosted. They included four World Cup matches in 1966 and the 1977 League Cup Final replay. The article added, 'It is a stadium that befits such occasions and the large crowds they attract.'

There was a huge amount of anticipation of what promised to be a great game. A New Year's Eve victory over Sheffield Wednesday, ironically at Hillsborough, had seen Forest embark on an eighteen-match unbeaten run, which gave their season a massive boost. They had reached two Wembley finals (both the Littlewoods and Simod cups) and this semi-final. In the match programme, Clough paid tribute to the players who had sparked hope of another era of success, to follow that which he enjoyed in the late 1970s. 'I am fifty-four and some would say I have shot it, but the players have kept me going – not only in recent weeks but in recent years,' he said. The England manager Bobby Robson (before he was knighted) predicted that the match would be one of the best semi-finals of all time. 'There will be so many good players on the pitch that I can't really see it being an anticlimax,' he said. But the harsh, dark reality of that sunny afternoon would cast a huge shadow over the whole country and led to a long campaign by the families of those innocent fans who died.

Liverpool: Grobbelaar, Ablet, Staunton, Nicol, Whelan, Hansen, Beardsley, Aldridge, Houghton, Barnes, McMahon.
Nottingham Forest: Sutton, Laws, Pearce, Walker, Wilson, Hodge, Gaynor, Webb, Clough, Chapman, Parker.

The match was a sell-out, meaning more than 53,000 fans from both sides made their way to Hillsborough. The arrangements for accommodating them were similar to those a year earlier, with Forest supporters occupying the Kop end and Liverpool fans in the Leppings Lane end, so they were positioned at the ends of the ground nearest their arrival points. In the book *Forever Forest*, Nottingham Forest's official historian, Don Wright, described what happened:

> Some 24,000 Liverpool fans had to be funnelled through just twenty-three turnstiles in the north and west sides of the ground. They could not cope before kick-off and when a crush developed outside police ordered an exit gate to be opened to admit hundreds of fans together. Undirected, they tried to get into the central Leppings Lane 'pens', which were already full.

On the pitch, the players were initially oblivious of the problems that were developing behind Bruce Grobbelaar's goal. At the other end of the pitch, a Liverpool corner led to Peter Beardsley volleying the ball against the Forest bar. Moments later, Forest's Brian Laws was about to take a throw-in on the right. It was a throw-in he would never take. As supporters spilled onto the pitch at the Liverpool end, trying to escape the crush, the match was stopped after six minutes by referee Ray Lewis and the players returned to the dressing rooms. Laws recalls in his autobiography, *Laws of the Jungle*, what happened next:

> There we were in suspended animation. It was all about trying to stay focussed on the game because even then we had no idea of the seriousness of the situation. Cloughie was sitting on the floor with his legs out, telling us to keep our minds on the job.

Laws said the referee came into the dressing room and said he would try to get the players back on the pitch. But when a police inspector entered shortly afterwards and suggested there may have been a fatality, Clough was adamant that the match should not continue. Clough's friend Colin Shields was sitting in the area of the directors' box. Like many others, he did not initially realise how serious the situation was. In his book *Champagne Memories*, Colin told me,

> I could see fans climbing over the side fences to try and escape, while others were being lifted by hand, by their fellow supporters, into the upper tier ... I could see police officers desperately trying to pull down the fencing to relieve the pressure that had built-up within the pens.

Trevor Frecknall of the *Nottingham Evening Post* reported how Clough and his opposite number Kenny Dalglish appeared on the touchline to be briefed by senior police officers. 'Both looked ashen-faced as they returned to the dressing rooms,' reported Frecknall. In his first autobiography, Clough's comments about the tragedy sparked controversy. While stating that the police had made serious errors of judgement and that innocent people had died, he also criticised the actions of some of the Liverpool supporters who, he said, had turned up later and in such numbers that mistakes were made. Clough said he was not accusing the Liverpool fans of being hooligans or hoodlums. But his criticisms were amplified when he appeared on the Clive Anderson television chat show as part of the publicity for the book.

Clough later made it clear that, like many others at the time, he had been misinformed. In his column for the magazine *Four Four Two* in November 2001, he said he had never intended to hurt anyone when commenting on the disaster. 'Now I've said some daft things in my time, but I hope most of them have been taken in the right spirit or at least a few have had a laugh at my expense,' he said. 'I now accept that I went too far in giving my opinions about Hillsborough.' Clough added that no malice had been intended but he accepted that many people on Merseyside hated the sight of him after what he had said. With that in mind, he thanked the Liverpool fans for the kindness they had shown his son Nigel who was playing for the club at the time of his father's comments. 'That showed the warmth and fairness of the folk on Merseyside,' said Clough before adding that he wanted to express his regret at the hurt he must have caused. In the same magazine column, he described his admiration for Liverpool's legendary manager Bill Shankly and said that for most of his own career in the top flight Liverpool had been the ultimate challenge. Clough said he was delighted that his teams had usually matched them. 'It's because of my love for Bill Shankly and his club's fantastic achievements that I respect Liverpool so much,' he said.

In 1991, the coroner at the original Hillsborough inquests, Dr Stefan Popper, said he would not hear any evidence relating to the deaths beyond 3.15 p.m. because he believed all the victims had died, or suffered fatal injuries, by then.

The deaths were ruled accidental. But those verdicts were quashed after the 2012 Hillsborough Independent Panel report and new hearings were ordered. It followed a long campaign by the families of those who died. They were determined to show that supporters were not responsible for causing the tragedy. New inquests in 2016 found that the ninety-six fans were unlawfully killed. It was official confirmation that fans were not to blame. The BBC reported how the jury found that the match commander, Chief Superintendent David Duckenfield, was 'responsible for manslaughter by gross negligence' due to a breach of his duty of care.

The semi-final between Liverpool and Forest was replayed at Old Trafford. Clough admitted he was full of apprehension about it. Brian Laws described it as a 'no-win situation' for Forest because nobody outside of Nottingham wanted to see them in the final. John Aldridge put Liverpool ahead but Forest drew level thanks to a goal from Neil Webb. After half-time, Aldridge made it 2-1 before Laws scored an own goal. As Laws sank to his knees, understandably devastated, Aldridge ruffled the full-back's hair. Many fans felt it showed a lack of respect that was uncalled for following the circumstances surrounding the replay. Clough was certainly unhappy about it and described Aldridge's actions as 'out of order'. Liverpool went on to beat their Merseyside neighbours Everton 3-2 in the final. As for Forest, they did manage to get to Wembley for the second time that season, lifting the Simod Cup after earlier success in the League Cup Final. But Clough said the awful events at Hillsborough would never be forgotten.

46

League Cup Final
Nottingham Forest 1 Oldham Athletic 0
29 April 1990

We got our hands on a cup again by playing the game the way it should be played.

By retaining the League Cup, Brian Clough demonstrated that he could not only create a team of trophy winners for the third time in his managerial career, but maintain that success too. After winning League Championships at Derby County in 1972 and Forest in 1978, as well as the European Cup and League Cup triumphs with the Reds, Clough saw his new crop of talented players lift more silverware by winning the Littlewoods Cup for the second successive season.

In the weeks leading up to the final, Clough was presented with his twenty-second Manager of the Month award, equalling Bob Paisley's record at Liverpool. During February 1990, Forest had remained unbeaten and secured their place in this final by beating Coventry City. Clough had also clocked-up his 1,000th League game as a manager, for which he received a magnum of champagne and an inscribed silver salver from the League sponsors.

Perhaps it was the 'curse' of the Manager of the Month award that meant Forest had a rocky time in the lead-up to the final. After six defeats and two draws they managed to turn the corner with a 3-0 win against Luton Town. But in their final game before Wembley, they suffered another defeat. This time they went down 2-0 at Southampton. Clough wondered whether it was the prospect of playing at the Twin Towers that had affected performances – 'pre-Wembleyitis' as he described it. He was thankful that they pulled themselves together in time for the big match.

Oldham Athletic: Rhodes, Irwin, Barlow, Henry, Barrett, Warhurst, Adams, Ritchie, Bunn, Milligan, Holden. Subs: Palmer, Williams.
Nottingham Forest: Sutton, Laws, Pearce, Walker, Chettle, Hodge, Crosby, Parker, Clough, Jemson, Carr. Subs: Wilson, Gaynor.

Attendance: 74,343

A goal by twenty-year-old Nigel Jemson early in the second half was enough to ensure Forest retained the trophy. Yet Oldham from Division Two had made a determined effort to take the lead. Andy Ritchie's 25-yard shot in the nineteenth minute looked destined for the top corner until Steve Sutton reached to push it over the bar. Sutton produced another superb save later in the second half. Paul Warhurt's long free-kick was nodded on by Ritchie to Roger Palmer, whose header appeared to be looping into the net. Forest's goalkeeper dived full length to his left to send the ball beyond the post and out for a corner.

The winning goal was created by Nigel Clough who picked out a gap in the Oldham defence and played a clever pass to Jemson. He raced clear of Earl Barrett and although the advancing Andy Rhodes blocked Jemson's initial shot, he could not prevent the striker scoring from the rebound. It capped a memorable season for Jemson who had made his debut on Boxing Day against Luton Town. Forest could have made it 2-0 in the closing minutes, when Stuart Pearce sent a 22-yard free-kick swerving around the defensive wall, but Rhodes dived to his right to push the ball away.

Clough applauded his players as Pearce collected the trophy. There was a double celebration for Des Walker because he not only had a winners' medal but also the inaugural Alan Hardaker Trophy for the Man of the Match. It had been named in memory of the man who had been instrumental in the introduction of the League Cup when he was secretary of the Football League. Clough said he intended to take the match ball home for his grandson Stephen. The manager said he had been pleased with how his players had performed during the season, producing flowing football in what he described as a nice manner. He said, 'We didn't try and kick anybody off the field, we didn't fall out with referees and we didn't moan when things went against us.'

47

FA Cup Final
Nottingham Forest 1
Tottenham Hotspur 2 (AET)
18 May 1991

I've got a taste for Wembley...

Much of the pre-match media coverage for this Wembley showpiece focused on the fact that the FA Cup was the one domestic trophy that had eluded Brian Clough. Over the previous twenty-six years in football management, Clough had seen his teams play more than eighty matches in the prestigious competition. Although those games had produced nearly forty victories, he had never reached the final – twice his Nottingham Forest side had made it to the semi-final stage against Liverpool and lost. This time, after a 4-0 semi-final win over West Ham, Clough's side faced Spurs.

The scale of what Clough had achieved at Forest, in finding, nurturing and motivating a fresh and successful side, was summed up by comparing the monetary value of his City Ground squad alongside the opponents from White Hart Lane. A report previewing the final, in the *Nottingham Evening Post*, pointed out that the Reds' line-up had been assembled for the footballing equivalent of loose change, while the Spurs team had been bought for nearly £9 million. A photograph to emphasise the point showed Lee Glover and Paul Gascoigne tussling for the ball during a previous match. Glover had joined frugal Forest for nothing from school, while Gazza had cost Spurs £2 million from Newcastle United. Clough's side had reached Wembley with an average age of twenty-three. Among them was nineteen-year-old Roy Keane. Said Clough, 'The biggest compliment I can pay Roy Keane is to say that the impact he's making reminds me of what Roy McFarland did when he came to Derby from Tranmere.'

When naming his team for the big day, Clough stayed loyal to the players who had won him a place in his first ever FA Cup Final. He selected the same eleven men who had beaten West Ham at Villa Park, which meant disappointment for England international Steve Hodge who was named as a substitute, while Keane was recalled after missing the previous league game due to injury. Right-back

Brian Laws also made way for Gary Charles who had missed the previous three league matches with a shoulder injury. In the official Wembley matchday programme, East Midlands Electricity took out a full-page advertisement to send a special message to the man who had appeared in their television and newspaper advertising campaigns. It read simply, 'Good luck Cloughie.' It was a sentiment echoed by many, usually neutral, observers who knew that a win for Clough would complete his trophy collection.

Nottingham Forest: Crossley, Charles, Pearce, Walker, Chettle, Keane, Crosby, Parker, Clough, Glover, Woan. Subs used: Laws, Hodge.
Spurs: Thorstvedt, Edinburgh, Van Den Hauwe, Sedgley, Howells, Mabbutt, Stewart, Gascoigne, Samways, Lineker, Allen. Subs used: Nayim, Walsh.

Attendance: 80,000

As Clough prepared to lead out his Forest team onto the Wembley turf, he wore a 'World's Greatest Grandpa' rosette on his grey jacket. 'Very smart,' commented the Spurs boss Terry Venables as the two managers chatted in the tunnel. When the time came to make their way across the pitch to the red carpet in front of the Royal Box, the noise in the stadium reached a new level and Clough grabbed the hand of Venables who was walking alongside him. Recalling that moment thirteen years later, Clough admitted he had felt nervous. He told *Four Four Two* magazine, 'Terry Venables said to me, "How can you be [nervous]? You've won everything!" I said, "But not the FA Cup – give us your hand." Terry saw the joke and that got rid of my nerves.'

Clough said he felt no nerves at all when he met Princess Diana a few minutes later. 'She told me, "I know who you are." I should think so too.' As the teams warmed up, Clough walked down the tunnel under the Royal Box so he could change into his working clothes: the familiar green jersey. The final had already kicked off by the time he took his seat on the bench, stopping on the way to hug a young supporter nearby.

Within the first fifteen minutes a hyper Gascoigne committed what Clough described as 'two despicable fouls'. The first was a chest-high challenge on Garry Parker, who still had the stud marks on his body after the match. It was the kind of shocking incident that deserved a red card, but referee Roger Milford did not even produce a yellow when he awarded a free-kick. Then there was a terrible knee-high lunge on Gary Charles. Again Gascoigne escaped punishment, but in committing the foul he injured himself so badly that he was soon stretchered off with ruptured knee ligaments. From the resulting free-kick, Forest captain Stuart Pearce launched a missile of a shot, which hammered its way into the top corner of the net before the Spurs wall could even turn around to see what had happened.

In his first autobiography, Clough reflected that he had wanted to see Gascoigne sent off for the first foul against Parker, never mind the one that led to him being carried from the field. The Forest boss said Milford should have brandished a red card over Gascoigne as he was carried off. It was a moment that seemed to influence the rest of the game. If Spurs had been reduced to ten men so early in the match, Forest's growing confidence while taking a 1-0 lead could have made a huge difference to the outcome. Instead, Venables sent on Nayim to replace Gascoigne, whose departure appeared to galvanise his teammates. Gary Lineker won a penalty after being brought down by Forest goalkeeper Mark Crossley before half-time. Crossley redeemed himself by diving to his left to push Lineker's spot-kick away.

At half-time there was a feeling among some fans that it could be Clough's day – a superb goal plus a penalty save suggested that the Reds' boss might complete his trophy collection. But Forest were struggling to execute their stylish passing game and the Spurs players appeared to become physically stronger as the match progressed. Among the Reds fans behind Crossley's goal in the first half was Richard Hallam, who admits he became increasingly doubtful that Clough could complete his set of cups. Richard recalls, 'Some games you get a feeling for how things are going to end up, and even after Pearce's goal and Crossley's penalty save, I remember thinking "we're not playing well here". It's a "bucket list" event going to an FA Cup Final, so at least that was achieved, and seeing Forest there was even better. It was old Wembley, of course, and I remember the view being decidedly questionable and the seat resembling a plastic brick. I hurt my shins on the one in front when Psycho scored. So much of the game against ten men might have been a different story.'

Ten minutes into the second half, Paul Allen found Paul Stewart racing in on the right side of the penalty area to equalise with an angled shot. The score remained level after ninety minutes, which meant half an hour of extra time would be needed. While Venables approached his players to offer encouragement, Clough remained seated on the bench and sent his backroom staff onto the pitch instead. It was a decision that surprised many. Wasn't this the moment when the master motivator could work his magic? Years later, Clough was adamant that he had done the right thing. After a gruelling ninety minutes, the players would not have wanted him to tell them anything, he said. 'At that stage I simply had nothing more to offer them.'

Early in extra time, Stewart flicked on a Nayim corner and Des Walker headed the ball into his own net. Clough was dignified in defeat, even giving Venables a kiss on the cheek. The *Nottingham Evening Post* reported that Clough smiled and vowed, 'I'll be back next year.' He said he had got a taste for Wembley, having been there four times in three years, and he would try to return the following season. In doing so, he dismissed speculation that he would retire. However, a few years later he admitted he should have retired after the cup final. But these things are easy to conclude in hindsight. The disappointing end to his incredible reign at the City Ground in 1993 could support the suggestion that he should have stepped down earlier, but having brought together a young and talented squad, the hunger for future success was understandable. Less than a month before the final the Forest chairman Maurice Roworth had told the media that Clough would be staying as manager whatever the result of the FA Cup Final. Roworth said that despite criticism from some fans about earlier results, Clough had done an excellent job for sixteen years and continued to be the boss that others looked up to with awe. The chairman added, 'Who else could have brought so much success to a club of our size?'

48

Premier League
Nottingham Forest 1 Liverpool 0
16 August 1992

You don't want roast beef and Yorkshire every night and twice on Sunday.

This Sunday afternoon 4 p.m. kick-off marked the start of a revolution in televised football: it was the first match of the new Premier League era to be shown live on Sky television. Every angle of the game was covered. 'Cameras sprang up like sniper positions,' reported the *Nottingham Evening Post*. 'Your bald patch could now be beamed around Britain by a bloke behind you in the Main Stand.' Also making its first appearance was the so-called 'Eyeball Express' that was actually a camera on rails along the length of one of the stands. One report said it had more success in catching Gary Crosby than Liverpool's David Burrows did.

Clough welcomed the cash that the television deal injected into the game, but he knew it was a double-edged sword. The timing of matches would often be dictated by television and he said later in the season that he did not like playing on Sunday afternoons. Neither did he welcome the prospect of Monday night games. Too much football – and too often – would be like having a Sunday dinner every day. Clough said other managers shared his concern about the number of matches being played and when they were held, and it was time their views were taken into consideration. He was also concerned about the quality of the Premier League and whether it would cause more wear and tear for players.

Sky's commentator Martin Tyler welcomed viewers by saying, 'Good afternoon, everyone. A new league, alterations and amendments to the very laws of the game, even a different button to push on your television set.' There was no doubt about it; television had taken over the City Ground. But as the *Nottingham Evening Post* pointed out, if you started to think you could run the show at Forest you soon ran into trouble. The unspoken rule among cameramen was to never stand in front of a certain man's dugout. However, one member of the satellite television crew made the classic error. 'He got away with a rocket from the real Boss of the City Ground,' added the newspaper. 'The next time he goes into Orbit!'

Nottingham Forest: Crossley, Laws, Pearce, Wilson, Chettle, Keane, Crosby, Gemmill, Clough, Sheringham, Woan. Subs: Marriott, Black, Bannister.
Liverpool: James, Tanner, Burrows, Nicol, Whelan, Wright, Saunders, Stewart, Rush, Walters, Thomas. Subs: Hooper, McManaman, Rosenthal.

Attendance: 20,038

Forest played like potential champions and dominated the first half. Mark Crossley did not have a shot to save in the first forty-five minutes, but his opposite number, David James, who was making his Liverpool debut, had a busy afternoon. As Forest piled on the pressure with neat, flowing football, a thunderous shot from Stuart Pearce was blocked by Mark Wright. It was only a matter of time before the home side got a goal and it came from a stunning drive by Teddy Sheringham. 'The first Premier League goal for Nottingham Forest – and it's a peach,' declared Sky's Martin Tyler.

Liverpool striker Ian Rush was substituted by Steve McManaman at half-time and the visitors had more possession in the second half. Although Crossley saved with his legs to stop a shot from Michael Thomas, Liverpool failed to find an equaliser. In fact, Forest could have gone further ahead when Roy Keane was brought down by James eight minutes from the end. But the referee decided not to award a penalty. Liverpool's defeat was the first time in eleven years that they had lost their opening fixture.

The Man of the Match was Teddy Sheringham, but he would play only two more matches for Forest before a transfer to Spurs. After such an impressive opening game, the Reds struggled to collect points and did not win again until eleven matches later. That was a 1-0 victory over Clough's hometown team Middlesbrough. Despite Clough's reservations about the impact of television, he gave an entertaining interview to the Sky reporter after the Liverpool game. When the interviewer finished by wishing him well for the campaign ahead, he replied, 'Young man, I hope to be seeing you a lot of times this season.'

49

Premier League
Nottingham Forest 0 Sheffield United 2
1 May 1993

As I said a couple of days ago, if I had one I would shoot my granny for three points.

It was an emotional afternoon at the City Ground as Brian Clough took charge of his final home League game after eighteen years as manager of Nottingham Forest. His side faced the prospect of relegation, but the thousands of fans inside the stadium were still determined to show their appreciation of his remarkable achievements. Although retirement was something he had been considering, it had been announced prematurely by the club amid speculation about the state of his health. Forest were second from bottom and Clough said it was important to put the side's Premier League safety ahead of his own farewell. The Reds had to win because United, fourth from bottom, had a superior goal difference.

Forest had struggled during the season and lost six matches in a row after winning the opening game against Liverpool. That run of defeats was brought to an end by a 1-1 draw with Coventry City in which Nigel Clough scored the equaliser and Roy Keane was a stand-in centre back. The failure to adequately replace striker Teddy Sheringham, whom Clough had allowed to join Spurs so he could be close to his young son, was a major factor in Forest's failing fortunes. Clough said he had become fed-up at hearing so many people say his side was 'too good to go down'. But one reader's letter in the *Nottingham Evening Post* summed-up what others feared. It started 'Forest won't go down … that's what they said about the Titanic'. Whether Forest would stay afloat depended on the result of the relegation decider against United. In the matchday programme, Clough admitted, 'The game is getting harder all the time but I'll summon one last effort in the hope that we can get the right results here this afternoon and against Ipswich next Saturday.'

As he walked down the tunnel and into the stadium, Clough was surrounded by photographers. Sitting in the stand opposite (it's now called the Brian

Clough Stand) I could feel the raw emotion of the Forest fans. I joined them in applauding my football hero who had brought us such enjoyable and unforgettable times. We were all willing him to succeed. He put both hands above his head as if to say 'thank you' for the reception he had received and even nodded in acknowledgement of the Sheffield United supporters. Having reached the dugout thanks to a police escort, he then kissed on the cheek each police officer who had shepherded him there. Now it was time for work.

Nottingham Forest: Marriott, Laws, Williams, Chettle, Tiler, Keane, Black, Gemmill, Clough, Rosario, Woan. Subs: Crossley, Stone, Orlygsson.
Sheffield United: Kelly, Ward, Beesley, Hartfield, Gayle, Pemberton, Bradshaw, Rogers, Hodges, Deane, Whitehouse. Subs: Carr, Leighton, Littlejohn.

Attendance: 26,752

The nerves of the Forest faithful were jangling when United thought they had won a penalty in the eighteenth minute. Glyn Hodges fell after a challenge from Brett Williams but referee Paul Durkin turned down the appeals. It was Hodges who broke the deadlock in the thirtieth minute. He latched onto a long clearance and curled a left-foot shot into the far corner. Forest almost equalised early in the second half when Brian Laws tried a shot from just outside the penalty area, but it went wide. The home side were fighting for their Premier League lives and went close again when Woan raced down the left and crossed for Roy Keane who was running towards the penalty spot. But Keane's header went wide. Forest's hopes of survival were finally ended when Brian Deane made it 2-0 with a header in the seventy-second minute. The Reds were dropping from the top flight for the first time in more than two decades. Nevertheless, the fans (including those in the away end) still showed their appreciation for Clough, who was standing beside the dugout in his familiar green jumper. He gave them a thumbs-up. Nothing more needed to be said.

After the final whistle, the supporters in the Trent end continued to sing his name and eventually he reappeared and walked onto the pitch as police officers tried to protect him. He was soon surrounded by fans who wanted to show how much they loved him. Brendan Hunt was one of the police officers on duty that day. In my book *The Day I Met Brian Clough* he said,

> I recall pushing through the crowd, who were making towards Brian, and with two or three other officers formed a police cordon around him, to offer him some protection from the crowd who were simply mobbing him. He looked tired and almost beaten, and perhaps a little overwhelmed. I said to him,

'Are you alright Brian?' and he replied, 'Oh yes, young man!' and he continued to conduct his pitch farewell.

Among the fans who were there that day was Rich Fisher, who was standing in the middle of the Trent End with his brother Alan. Rich recalls going onto the pitch to get close to Clough. 'It was very special,' he said. 'It was one last chance to show what he meant to us.' Despite what had been a terrible season, it was vital to give him a tremendous send-off. Added Rich, 'I can't think of any other sport where that has happened. It speaks volumes for the depth of love that Forest fans had for him.'

The matchday programme for the game against United had a special cover that featured photographs of Clough and the message, 'Thanks for the Memories'. Inside it, he told the fans he had spent nearly a third of his life at the City Ground and while there had been ups and downs (mostly ups, he added) they had been lovely to him 'all along the line'. He ended his column in the programme with the words, 'Be good ... and thanks for having me.'

50

County Cup Final
Nottingham Forest 3 Notts County 0
11 May 1993

I wouldn't say I was the best manager in the business, but I was in the top one.

The Nottingham Forest matchday programme described it as 'The Final Curtain'. It was Brian Clough's last first-team match as a manager. Alongside a photograph of him, an item in the programme said that although the occasion may not be spiced with the magic of Munich or Madrid, Clough would still cherish one more trophy triumph. Fittingly, the article added that victory in Nottinghamshire's own 'cup final' would give him the chance to bow out in the way he would be best remembered in the future, by placing one final piece of silverware in the trophy cabinet. The man himself told the press, 'We'll approach it as we always do. No fuss – just trying to win.'

Despite Clough's comments, there was plenty of fuss on the night. The headline on the back page of the *Nottingham Evening Post* declared, 'Ovation to The Master,' next to a photograph of him blowing a kiss to the crowd. It was described as his 'final Forest kiss'. Thousands of fans went onto the pitch after the game to give him a ten-minute standing ovation.

A few days before the match, there had been another standing ovation at Ipswich in his final League game. Ipswich's general manager John Lyall presented his old friend with an inscribed silver salver in recognition of his achievements. Clough also collected cards and flowers from well-wishers before giving his traditional thumbs-up to the Forest fans who had travelled to Portman Road. His son Nigel scored a penalty in a 2-1 defeat by the club he had made his debut against nine years earlier.

Brian Clough said that after a disappointing season, it would be nice to finish by winning a cup. According to the manager, although some people might have thought the County Cup was not important to Forest, there was no such thing as a non-important match. Whether it was a testimonial game or a European Cup Final, he had always taken the same approach. 'It's stood me in good stead for a few years and I've not done that badly because I've won a fair few matches and collected the odd trophy along the way,' he said. Clough added that he always enjoyed matches against Notts County and hoped that at some point in the future both clubs would be together in the Premier League. 'It increases the interest around the place and it helps to put a few bums on seats as well,' he told the matchday programme.

Nottingham Forest: Marriott, Laws, Williams, Chettle, Tiler, Keane, Black, Gemmill, Clough, Glover, Woan. Subs: Crossley, Stone, Orlygsson, McKinnon, Armstrong.
Notts County: Cherry, Turner, Walker, Wilson, Cox, Thomas, Worboys, Draper, Reeves, Devlin, Agana. Subs: Short, Wells, Catlin, Slawson.

Forest had most of the possession and created the majority of chances during the game, but it remained goalless until the sixty-third minute. Then, Nigel Clough found Scot Gemmill with a lovely pass and the midfielder put Forest ahead. A few minutes later, Lee Glover shot from 12 yards to make it 2-0. The Reds' third goal was a header by Kingsley Black. Defender Carl Tiler suffered a knee injury and was substituted by Steve Stone. After the final whistle the cup was collected by Nigel Clough and Roy Keane. It was a fitting way to end. Clough had put another trophy in the cabinet.

It is probably fair to say that it was only after Clough had savoured the adulation of the City Ground for the last time that his remarkable achievements were fully appreciated. As a report in the *Nottingham Evening Post* stated, 'In the true spirit of never knowing a good thing until it's lost, the end of an amazing era will only serve to enhance the legend.' In a brilliant tribute to the Master Manager, the newspaper said that just as time BC – Before Clough – had been virtually obliterated from the memories by a host of medals and balmy nights of European glory, time AC would magnify his every success.

When Frank Clark was announced as his successor, Clough described him as the best choice for the job. 'He's got grace and he's reliable, warm and charming,' said Clough. 'I hope he also brings his guitar because I love music and he plays it well.' Clough added that he might even leave Clark one of his Frank Sinatra tapes. Clark had expertise and experience, said Clough, whose only piece of advice was not to let directors on the team coach. 'In twenty-odd years of management, that's a rule I've maintained.'

While Clough redefined the art of football management, his playing career must be remembered too. In 2004, just a few months before he passed away, Clough told *Four Four Two* magazine, 'Nothing I did in the rest of my career compares with being young, fit and scoring goals by the barrowload. Management is only a substitute for playing football.' There is no doubt that

Brian Clough's incredible achievements as both a player and a manager will never be forgotten.

* * *

Brian Clough died on 20 September 2004 at the age of sixty-nine. A memorial service was attended by around 15,000 people. Fans can see statues of him in Nottingham, Derby and Middlesbrough. He was made a Freeman of Nottingham in 1993 and of Derby ten years later. In his memory, he was inducted into the National Football Museum's European Hall of Fame in 2008. To mark the occasion, his son Nigel received an award on his father's behalf and described it as a huge honour.

* * *

Send memories of your favourite Clough match, for possible future publication, to youngman@brianclough.com

Bibliography

Clough The Autobiography, Brian Clough with John Sadler, Transworld Publishers Ltd, London, 1994.

Walking on Water, Brian Clough, Headline Book Publishing, London, 2002.

Forest Giants, John McGovern & Rob Jovanovic, Pineapple Books Ltd, Nottingham, 2003.

Brian Clough's Book of Football, Brian Clough & John Lawson, Stafford Pemberton Publishing Ltd, Knutsford, Cheshire, 1981.

The Day I Met Brian Clough, Marcus Alton, DB Publishing, Derby, 2011.

The Life of Brian, Tim Crane, Football World, footballworld.co.uk, 2004.

Nottingham Forest – The Official Statistical History, Ken Smales, Pineapple Books Ltd, Nottingham, 2006.

Forest 1865–1978, John Lawson, Wensum Books Ltd, Norwich, 1978.

Forest – The 1979 Season, John Lawson, Wensum Books Ltd, Norwich, 1979.

Nottingham Forest Annual 1979, Dave Horridge, Circle Publications Ltd, Ilford, Essex, 1978.

Forever Forest, Don Wright, Amberley Publishing, Stroud, Gloucestershire, 2015.

Super Tramp, John Robertson with John Lawson, Mainstream Publishing Company, Edinburgh, 2011.

From Bo'ness to the Bernabeu, John McGovern and Kevin Brennan, Vision Sports Publishing, Kingston upon Thames, 2012.

My Magic Carpet Ride, Garry Birtles, Reid Publishing, Loughborough, Leicestershire, 2010.

Laws of the Jungle, Brian Laws with Alan Biggs, verticaleditions.com, 2012.

Champagne Memories, Colin Shields with Marcus Alton, DB Publishing, Nottingham, 2014.

His Way, Patrick Murphy, Robson Books, London, 2004.

The Official History of Nottingham Forest, Philip Soar, Polar Publishing, Leicester, 1998.

Nottingham Forest FC Official Handbook 1990–91 Volume Two, Julian Baskcomb and John *Lawson*, ACL Colour Print & Polar Publishing Ltd, Leicester, 1990.

The Big Matches, Brian Moore & Martin Tyler, Queen Anne Press, London, 1980.

Middlesbrough Football Club, Eric Paylor, Archive Publications Ltd, 1989.

The Lads in the Sixties (Sunderland in the Golden Decade of English Football), Alan Brett and Philip Curtis, Black Cat Publications, Sunderland, 2008.

Sunderland Til I Die (The People's History), Alan Brett and Andrew Clark, The People's History Ltd, 1999.

The Definitive Hartlepool United FC, Gordon Small, Tony Brown (Publisher), Nottingham, 1998

Hartlepool United: The Complete Record, Malcolm Errington, The Derby Books Publishing Company Ltd, Derby, 2012.

The Official History of Hartlepool United Football Club (limited edition), Hartlepool United FC, 2009.

The Real Mackay, Dave Mackay with Martin Knight, Mainstream Publishing Company (Edinburgh) Ltd, 2004.

Right Place Right Time, George Edwards, Tempus Publishing, Stroud, 2007.

There Was Some Football Too... (100 Years of Derby County), Tony Francis, Queen Anne Press, London, for Derby County FC, 1984.

brianclough.com

11v11.com

thegoldstonewrap.com

safc.com

worldfootball.net

poolstats.co.uk

thenorthernecho.co.uk

europeancuphistory.com

hotspurhq.com

inthemadcrowd.co.uk

mightyleeds.co.uk

bbc.co.uk/news

Champions of Europe – 25 Years On (DVD), The Media Group (Exec Producer Keith Daniell, Director Andrew James)

Cloughie – The Brian Clough Story (video), Watershed Pictures (Exec Producer Grant Bovey)

Tyne Tees Television

Nottingham Forest matchday programmes

Four Four Two magazine

BBC *Match of the Day* magazine

North Eastern Evening Gazette
Middlesbrough Gazette
Sunderland Echo
The Northern Echo
Northern Daily Mail
Hartlepool Mail
Observer Sport Monthly
Derby Evening Telegraph
Nottingham Evening Post
Football Post
Brighton Argus
Cambridge News
The Sun
The Daily Mail
The Daily Mirror
The Sunday Mirror
The Guardian
The Sunday Times

About the Author

Marcus Alton is an award-winning journalist and editor of the tribute website brianclough.com. He has worked for the BBC for nearly thirty years but began his career as a news and sports reporter on the *Newark Advertiser,* where he was named Midlands Sports Reporter of the Year.

He has written three other books about Brian Clough, *Young Man, You've Made My Day, Champagne Memories,* and *The Day I Met Brian Clough,* which includes memories from his family, friends and fans. He also wrote 'A View from the Brian Clough Stand', a regular column in the Nottingham Forest matchday programme.

Marcus interviewed Cloughie several times and in August 2000 set up the non-profit making tribute website, which has the backing of the Clough family. He instigated the campaign for a bronze statue of Brian in Nottingham, forming a committee of volunteers who smashed their fundraising target in just eighteen months. The statue was unveild by Barbara Clough in Novemeber 2008.